New World Pope

†

STUDIES IN WORLD CATHOLICISM

New World Pope

Pope Francis and the Future of the Church

EDITED BY
Michael L. Budde

CONTRIBUTORS

Francesca Ambrogetti
Ann W. Astell
Peter J. Bernardi, SJ
Maria Clara Lucchetti Bingemer
Allan Figueroa Deck, SJ
Francis Cardinal George, OMI
Barbara E. Reid, OP
Sergio Rubin
Abraham Skorka
Andrea Tornielli

CASCADE *Books* · Eugene, Oregon

NEW WORLD POPE
Pope Francis and the Future of the Church

Studies in World Catholicism 2

Copyright © 2017 Wipf and Stock Publishers. All rights reserved. Except for brief quotations in critical publications or reviews, no part of this book may be reproduced in any manner without prior written permission from the publisher. Write: Permissions, Wipf and Stock Publishers, 199 W. 8th Ave., Suite 3, Eugene, OR 97401.

Cascade Books
An Imprint of Wipf and Stock Publishers
199 W. 8th Ave., Suite 3
Eugene, OR 97401

www.wipfandstock.com

PAPERBACK ISBN: 978-1-4982-8371-7
HARDCOVER ISBN: 978-1-4982-8373-1
EBOOK ISBN: 978-1-4982-8372-4

Cataloguing-in-Publication data:

Names: Budde, Michael L., editor.

Title: New world pope : Pope Francis and the future of the church / edited by Michael L. Budde.

Description: Eugene, OR : Cascade Books, 2017 | Series: Studies in World Catholicism 2 | Includes bibliographical references and index.

Identifiers: ISBN 978-1-4982-8371-7 (paperback) | ISBN 978-1-4982-8373-1 (hardcover) | ISBN 978-1-4982-8372-4 (ebook)

Subjects: LCSH: Francis, Pope, 1936– | Catholic Church—History—21st century.

Classification: BX1378.7 .N48 2017 (print) | BX1378.7 .N48 (ebook)

Manufactured in the U.S.A.   06/01/17

English translation of "Francis: Renovator, Reformer, or Revolutionary?" ©2016 by Karen M. Kraft. Used with permission.

Scripture quotations marked (NRSV) are from New Revised Standard Version Bible, copyright © 1989 National Council of the Churches of Christ in the United States of America. Used by permission. All rights reserved worldwide.

Scripture texts in chapter 6 of this work are taken from the New American Bible, revised edition © 2010, 1991, 1986, 1970 Confraternity of Christian Doctrine, Washington, D.C. and are used by permission of the copyright owner. All Rights Reserved. No part of the New American Bible may be reproduced in any form without permission in writing from the copyright owner.

Contents

Acknowledgments | vii

Introduction by Michael L. Budde | ix

1. Reflections on Pope Francis and the Future of the Church | 1
   —Francis Cardinal George, OMI

2. Foot Washing: Reflections on the Fourth Gospel and the Exemplary Leadership of Pope Francis | 9
   —Barbara E. Reid, OP

3. The Next Step | 24
   —Abraham Skorka

4. Understanding Pope Francis: Roots and Horizons of Church Reform | 35
   —Allen Figueroa Deck, SJ

5. Pope Francis and Ignatian Discernment | 53
   —Peter J. Bernardi, SJ

6. Pope Francis, the Ecclesial Movements, and the New Evangelization | 70
   —Ann W. Astell

7. The Hope of a Future for the Catholic Church | 86
   —Maria Clara Lucchetti Bingemer

8. A Journalist's Notes on Pope Francis and His Testimony: The Call to the Worldwide Church for "Pastoral Conversion" | 98
   —Andrea Tornielli

9. Francis: Renovator, Reformer, or Revolutionary? Two Reflections | 107
   —Sergio Rubin and Francesca Ambrogetti

Bibliography | 115

Subject Index | 123

Scripture Index | 129

Acknowledgments

Many people helped bring this book to life, and to make it better than it would have been otherwise. Foremost among them is Karen Kraft, the communications coordinator for DePaul University's Center for World Catholicism and Intercultural Theology (CWCIT). Her skills as a translator, editor, and overseer allow the Center to initiate and disseminate theological scholarship from and for a worldwide audience; her patience and good cheer are tested on a regular basis, yet thus far have emerged triumphant.

This book is also built upon the good cheer and expertise of Francis Salinel, the Center's administrative coordinator. Like Karen, Francis combines substantive theological knowledge of many sorts with logistical efficiency and competence. In addition, this book has benefited from the assistance and support of Brenda Washington, administrative coordinator for DePaul's Department of Catholic Studies, in which the Center is housed.

These chapters first saw light of day as presentations at the Center's 2014 conference, "New World Pope: Pope Francis and the Future of the Church." This gathering, like all of the Center's activities, was possible thanks to benefactors and supporters both within and beyond DePaul University. The former include the Department of Catholic Studies, the College of Liberal Arts and Social Sciences, and the Office of Academic Affairs. The latter includes Wipf and Stock Publishers, whose Cascade Books division is our partner in producing Studies in World Catholicism, the book series of which this volume is a part; we are grateful for their expertise and many strengths.

Introduction

MICHAEL L. BUDDE

One need not be a pollster, nor a cultural savant, to know that Pope Francis is big news. Since becoming pope in 2013, the former Jorge Mario Bergoglio has taken the world by storm—his candor, his wit, his compassion, his ability to confound expectations and stereotypes—and the world has responded by following his every gesture, word, and action.

The publishing world has seen an explosion in titles about this leader of the Catholic Church. Theologians, journalists, historians, former colleagues, church critics, scientists, and more—all have found Francis to be a character worth investigating, interrogating, or getting to know. So many books have emerged in the first few years that it almost seems as if any new book on Pope Francis should justify its existence in advance.

This is another book on Pope Francis, and here is its justification. This book has no pictures of the pontiff, no amusing anecdotes from his public appearances, not many heartwarming stories about his childhood adventures and boyhood pranks. It spends relatively little time elevating Francis by denigrating his predecessors, although it does note where Francis is moving in new directions and with different emphases. It resists the urge to indulge in wild speculation about improbable future events, revolutions, and conspiracies.

What this book does, what it hopes to contribute to discussions within the Christian world, within the academy, and among the general public, relates to the roots of Pope Francis's thoughts. From where come his ideas about God, about the social mission of the Church, about the imperatives for discipleship and the centrality of joy? Where did this unusual Argentinian find his inspiration, what formed his convictions, and what foundations undergird his vision for the Church's future?

It matters that Pope Francis was formed by and lived within the world of the Society of Jesus—the Jesuits, the religious order founded by Ignatius of Loyola in the sixteenth century. It matters that Francis was raised the son of Italian immigrants in Argentina, a cosmopolitan crossroads in Latin America with a recent history of labor activism and progressive politics as well as brutal authoritarianism and repression. It matters that he is a product of the Second Vatican Council, the profound reform of Catholicism (1962–65) whose energies are not yet exhausted.

All of this matters to persons interested in the integrity of the Gospel and its future around the world. This book seeks to contribute to the conversation on the future of the Church led by Francis by looking back to the roots of the vision he represents. Doing so requires looking beyond the person of Francis himself, beyond the persona created for and about him by countless interpreters and observers—indeed, looking beyond Francis to larger and deeper matters is precisely what Francis himself seeks. One suspects that he sees his celebrity in instrumental terms—unimportant in itself, but perhaps useful in directing people to encounters with Christ and His mission in the world. These encounters, as Francis has suggested, can set the world on fire with love in the most unexpected ways and places—the affable old man has revolutionary objectives for church and world that far exceed his lifespan.

An exploration like this is best done by a community of scholars, from a variety of starting points and disciplines, coming together to share their findings and insights as well as challenging one another's conclusions. Such a gathering was organized in February 2014 by the Center for World Catholicism and Intercultural Theology (CWCIT)—a research center sponsored by DePaul University in Chicago focused on the worldwide nature of the Catholic communion, especially in the so-called global South of Latin America, Africa, and Asia. A small group of scholars, church leaders, and journalists gathered to share work on where Bergoglio comes from—his understanding of theology, the influence on him from scripture, the legacy of the Jesuits, and the political realities of poverty and oppression that define much of the world. Some of the contributors are Jesuits who explore how Ignatian spirituality informs the life and ministry of Pope Francis;

some are scholars who have explored the influences that have shaped him and his views on God, Jesus, and the world; some are journalists who have had unfiltered access to him and to important people in his life; one is among the cardinals who elected Bergoglio as pope, and one is a rabbi who has been a close friend of Pope Francis for several decades. You will not find discussion here of Pope Francis's encyclical on the environment—that project had not been announced when this group gathered—but you will learn why that later project made sense given who Francis is and where his journey through life has taken him.

The Making of Pope Francis

It is fitting to start discussing the "making of Pope Francis" with remarks from one of the people who "made" Pope Francis. As a member of the College of Cardinals, the electoral college of Catholic leaders who gathered to select a successor to Pope Benedict XVI, Francis Cardinal George of Chicago was unusually well placed to discuss why the Catholic leadership believed that the Holy Spirit led them to select this man, at this time.

The cardinals knew that the times required someone who would, at a minimum, improve ecclesiastical governance—especially by way of reforming the Curia, or the permanent bureaucracy that carries out the functions of the Vatican. But they wanted more than just an administrator—as Cardinal George notes, the cardinals wanted someone "who knows how to govern and someone who has a heart for the poor" (3)—traits often in short supply on their own, still less so when joined. Writing fourteen months before his death from cancer, Cardinal George noted that even after it was clear that Bergoglio was to be selected the next pope, nevertheless "the Spirit is a Spirit of surprises" (5)—the immediate surprises included the name Bergoglio selected for his pontificate (no one had ever dared to name himself after Saint Francis of Assisi before), the free-spiritedness of the new pope, his appreciation for images and gestures, and "a populist approach to his ministry," something that "wasn't evident in Buenos Aires" (5).

Cardinal George provides an interesting first-person account of the process by which the cardinals converse, get to know one another, and share their hopes for the church (as well as their prayers that God will guide their discernment rather than their own partial agendas). It reveals the qualities they hoped to find in the new leader for the world's Catholics—and it is leadership that draws the attention of Barbara Reid, for whom Pope Francis presents a manual for leadership quite different from those presented in the seemingly unending corpus of "leadership studies."

An internationally renowned New Testament scholar, Reid begins her reflections with one of the first iconic expressions of Pope Francis's leadership style—his washing the feet of inmates at a Holy Thursday worship service in a juvenile detention center. While this expression of servant leadership has been part of the papal celebration of Holy Week in years past, Pope Francis added his own distinctive elements—especially washing the feet of women and Muslims—only twelve days into his term as pope. Reid reviews the literature on the theology of foot washing in the Christian tradition and identifies seven features as being most relevant—perhaps together constituting a schematic for Christian leadership rightly understood. She finds the Gospel of John especially fruitful in explicating Pope Francis's understanding of love, service, and sacrifice as the signal qualities of following Christ.

> In expounding on the joy of the Gospel, Pope Francis adopts a theology evident in the Gospel of John, which stresses the centrality of divine love, not atonement for sin. In his exhortation at the end of the Way of the Cross at World Youth Day in Rio de Janeiro in July 2013, he made this most explicit. He exhorted the young people, "The cross of Christ is an invitation for us to fall in love with him and to then reach out and help our neighbors . . . The cross gives us an assurance of the unshakable love which God has for us . . . a love so great that it enters into our sin and forgives it, enters into our suffering and gives us the strength to bear it. It is a love which enters into death to conquer it and to save us . . . Jesus's cross contains "all the love of God, his immeasurable mercy." (22)

Loving relationships are of several types; one of special relevance to Christianity is that of friendship, one especially important in John's Gospel (e.g., 15:15; 21:5). How fitting, then, to have a contribution from one of Pope Francis's lifelong friends—Rabbi Abraham Skorka, with whom the pope has written a book[1] and with whom he worked on interfaith and Jewish-Christian concerns for several decades.

In "The Next Step," Rabbi Skorka reviews the long and generally depressing history of Jewish-Christian relations, the challenges to Christianity presented by the Shoah, and postwar initiatives by the Catholic Church

---

1. Bergoglio and Skorka, *On Heaven and Earth: Pope Francis on Faith, Family and the Church in the Twenty-First Century.*

to rid itself of the sins of anti-Semitism and anti-Judaism. He highlights the many voices in Christian-Jewish dialogue and the possibilities of such; he also highlights the eschatological nature of this relationship, when God will gather the whole world back to Him and show what each of the two peoples had to contribute. Skorka offers a rich and nuanced sampler of major Jewish theological voices and views (not all in agreement with one another), all reflecting the creative engagement of God with His people (and those aspiring to be his adopted children). As he notes,

> The future of Christian-Jewish dialogue lies in resuming, and renewing, the old dialogue, which was disrupted almost two thousand years ago. Of course, it is impossible to restart the dialogue at the same point at which it was broken off and disregard all that happened during the succeeding two thousand years. But the challenge for each side is to see the other as a partner in the struggle of a common challenge: to install a dimension of spirituality in the midst of humanity, erasing idolatry in all its forms from human reality. (33)

Skorka reinforces the point by referencing Abraham Joshua Heschel: "Nazism has suffered a defeat, but the process of eliminating the Bible from the consciousness of the Western world goes on. It is on this issue of saving the radiance of the Hebrew Bible in the minds of man [sic] that Jews and Christians are called upon to work together. *None of us can do it alone*" (34).

One can see that Bergoglio has had a learned, critical, and generous friend and partner in his theological journey. It helps account for Pope Francis's willingness to criticize the wrong turns and sins in Christian history, his commitment to interreligious partnership, and his embrace of honest disagreements within the overarching bonds of love and friendship.

The affinities between rabbinic reasoning and Jesuit sensibilities have been remarked upon more than once, and it is fitting that Rabbi Skorka's role in Pope Francis's life would build upon and engage the Ignatian roots of his intellectual and spiritual formation. The pope's Ignatian formation and sensibilities are some of what is explored in depth by his Jesuit colleagues Allan Figueroa Deck and Peter Bernardi.

In "Understanding Pope Francis: Roots and Horizons of Church Reform," Deck suggests that identifying some of the "sources" of this pope might provide some insights regarding his likely future directions. In addition to Francis's Jesuit formation, Deck suggests that other key factors in shaping his priorities and convictions include being born to Italian immigrants in Argentina; the ecclesial context he experienced in Argentina; the power of the "theology of the people" as lived in the region; his experiences as archbishop of Buenos Aires; and his leadership role in the Aparecida Conference in May 2007. All of this has shaped the pope's pastoral vision, and suggests that some roads ahead are more likely than others.

Deck's emphasis on the profoundly urban nature of Bergoglio's experiences is important:

> Perhaps no other pope in history is the product of an immense, cosmopolitan urban environment like that of greater Buenos Aires, one of the ten most densely populated urban centers of the world, and certainly among the top—if not the top—cultural and artistic centers of Latin America. Argentina has a long history of immigration and is, along with Brazil, the most culturally diverse nation of Latin America. While firmly Catholic in tradition, Argentina—this is true of Buenos Aires in particular—is also ecumenical and interreligious, with thriving churches of various Christian denominations, Islamic mosques, and Jewish synagogues. It is also a significantly secular city, even though Catholic history and symbolic expressions are omnipresent. (37)

Deck's deep familiarity with the Spanish-language sources on Francis is a decided advantage to his research and to his readers; Deck's analysis is a useful corrective to some criticisms of Pope Francis that suggest the pontiff brings into church life nothing more than an unreflective Peronism easily categorized and dismissed.

For his part, Bernardi highlights the ways in which the Jesuit Bergoglio has been shaped by having both performed and directed the "Long Retreat" of St. Ignatius—a thirty-day experience of the Spiritual Exercises. Bernardi describes the Exercises as "an ordered series of meditations and contemplation grounded in Scripture that draw the retreatant into a profound encounter with Christ" (56). The experience is divided into four one-week sections, focusing on consideration of sin and the mercy of God; the life of Christ up to Palm Sunday; the passion and death of Christ; and Christ's resurrection and ascension. A person shaped by these experiences is better equipped to see God in all things, a disposition that requires both patience and humility. Bernardi quotes Pope Francis on this need for humility:

> If a person says that he met God with total certainty and is not touched by a margin of uncertainty, then this is not good. For me, this is an important key. If one has all the answers to all the questions—that is the proof that God is not with him. It means

that he is a false prophet using religion for himself. The great leaders of the people of God, like Moses, have always left room for doubt. You must leave room for the Lord, not for our certainties; we must be humble. (59)

Bernardi here provides a concise but wide-ranging exploration of the Christian missionary impulse as embedded in the Jesuit tradition; such ranges from matters of church leadership and clericalism to the summons to all baptized Christians to risk mistakes and errors in the adventure that is loving the world and following Christ.

While Pope Francis remains a Jesuit through and through, his spirituality and hope for the church has long been open to other ecclesial channels and traditions. Historian Ann Astell, in "Pope Francis, the Ecclesial Movements, and the New Evangelization," provides an important exploration of how contemporary movements within the Church have been understood by the pontiff.

While at least some of Francis's initial popularity built upon an exaggerated contrast between him and his papal predecessors (heavy-handed and authoritarian John Paul and Benedict, personable and inclusive Francis), Astell is correct in noting the shared appreciation all three have for the new movements that have emerged in the last several decades. She also explores, however, the ways in which Francis's understanding of these movements differs from those of earlier popes. Specifically, Pope Francis not only blesses and supports these movements, but he has also participated in some of them; in addition, his missionary ideas about the church have much in common with the evangelizing objectives of several of the movements. As Astell notes, Francis develops the Marian implications of the movements—rendering (and recommending to the rest of us) a picture of Mary as the first witness and great missionary, a style that is both merciful and joyful.

A sense of joy undergirds much of the popular reception of Pope Francis's election, notes Brazilian theologian Maria Clara Lucchetti Bingemer. She testifies to the hope and delight taken by church people for whom Pope John XXIII was a central figure, and for whom Vatican II became a promise unfulfilled in the decades that followed. In "The Hope of a Future for the Catholic Church," she identifies several elements of Vatican II that will see more development under Pope Francis: ecumenism and interreligious dialogue, ecclesial collegiality, and liturgical reform.

She also sees a "return to the poor" as both the content and method of Francis's theology. As she notes, "Francis does not forget and does not allow anyone to forget at whose service the Church is, in charity. Faithful to the Gospel, he proclaims that the ones the world considers least are actually the most beloved by God, His preferred ones. Therefore, they should be the first and preferential option of Christ's Church" (87).

Bingemer speaks both of the ecclesial and popular reception of Bergoglio's elevation to the papacy, and the ways in which people came to learn about his past and aspirations. One of the most distinctive things about Pope Francis's leadership style to date has been his openness to journalists, religious and secular alike—through them the world has come to know his plain-speaking style, his disarming humility, and his sense of humor. He has made his humanity central to his repositioning of the Church—far from clerical pretentions and churchy triumphalism, willing to critique itself in order to better meet the needs of the world and the most vulnerable therein.

It is fitting, therefore, that the last word in this volume goes to journalists who have done so much to bring his person and mission to audiences around the world—ranging far beyond those ordinarily interested in what popes say or do.

Andrea Tornielli, a reporter with the Italian daily *La Stampa*, is among those reporters who have conducted extensive interviews with Pope Francis. In "A Journalist's Notes on Pope Francis and His Testimony: The Call to the Worldwide Church for 'Pastoral Conversion,'" Tornielli shares reflections on what he came to learn about his unusually accessible and uninhibited leader.

Among other things, Tornielli reminds us that while Pope Francis has made headlines with his major pronouncements and documents, it is in his everyday preaching that one often finds the deepest insights into his passions and desires for God's people. Sometimes these make their way into the secular media, as happened with his comments on the Vigil of Pentecost in 2013:

> If we step outside ourselves we find poverty. Today—it sickens the heart to say so—the discovery of a tramp who has died of the cold is not news . . . Today, the thought that a great many children do not have food to eat is not news. This is serious, this is serious! We cannot put up with this! Yet that is how things are. We cannot become starched Christians, those overeducated Christians who speak of theological matters as they calmly sip their tea. No!

> We must become courageous Christians and go in search of the people who are the very flesh of Christ, those who are the flesh of Christ! (102)

For their part, Sergio Rubin and Francesca Ambrogetti conducted a series of interviews over a two-year period that were published in English in 2013 as *Pope Francis: Conversations with Jose Bergoglio*. They both offered thoughts on "Pope Francis: Renovator, Reformer, or Revolutionary?"

Rubin says that the public has come to understand that Pope Francis is about change, but what sort of change? Of what magnitude? The pope is about change of several sorts, according to Rubin. He is a renovator, in the sense of generating "renewed enthusiasm among the faithful." Is he a reformer? Not in terms of changing church teaching, but rather in terms of changing church practices and disciplines. He is decidedly a revolutionary—not in a negative sense, but inasmuch as he is "carrying out a kind of cultural revolution in the Church. Because, in my opinion, after centuries during which the institution seemed to favor guilt and condemnation (or, at least, that's how a good part of society perceived it), Francis is returning love to its place front and center" (109).

Ambrogetti sees this revolution as one aimed at the human conscience, which she sees as "the most difficult of all places" (111). She notes the priorities that seemed to motivate those who voted for Bergoglio to be pope, and how Pope Francis is approaching these concerns.

The key question, says Rubin, is whether the faithful will join him in renovation, reform, and revolution. "Will they merely applaud him, or will they actually follow him?" (110). Good questions indeed, the answers to which will likely be central to how the church and world of the future understand the legacy of Pope Francis.

1

Reflections on Pope Francis and the Future of the Church

FRANCIS CARDINAL GEORGE, OMI

Thank you very much. I am grateful to all of you for being part of this conference, and grateful to the university and Fr. Holtschneider for beginning this initiative some years ago and, before that, for also beginning the Catholic Studies Program at DePaul. These initiatives have done a lot to reposition the study of the Catholic faith within DePaul University's programs. The role that I agreed to play this morning was just to say a few words about the circumstances of the pope's election, the way in which he has followed the program that was anticipated, and the way in which he surprised us by not doing so.

    A year ago, when we went into conclave because Benedict XVI had resigned the papal office—which was an extraordinary event born of his own freedom—we were well aware that the reason he gave for his resignation was the strain on him to the point that he felt he couldn't really adequately fulfill the office, do what needed to be done for the sake of the Church. He resigned for love of the Church. Part of the difficulty was his health condition. He had warned us about that before the election eight years ago (nine years ago now). The heart condition that is trying to him was already known; the doctors discouraged him from flying for that reason. Also, his personality is very different from that of Pope John Paul II's, and he pointed that out as well. He is a scholar who spent much of his life in a classroom and in libraries before he was made the archbishop of Munich. For four years he governed a local church and then he returned basically to scholarly pursuits as head of the Congregation of the Doctrine of the Faith. He did a wonderful job there and was, as we all know, someone who helped Pope John Paul II create a magisterium that incorporated contemporary philosophical concerns, particularly subjectivity from the phenomenological school, into Thomism and the more classical theological way of expressing the faith. The magisterium of John Paul II was quite original in many ways. People think of him as a traditionalist, which he is, but it is a tradition that is alive, and future generations will sort it out in ways that will show just how original his mind truly was. Part of John Paul's program was, of course, possible because of the work of Cardinal Ratzinger, who is so immersed in the Fathers of the Church and in the theological tradition. When the cardinals met, still grieving, at the death of a truly monumental figure, Pope John Paul II, the concern was to continue his legacy in some fashion. The obvious person who could do that was Joseph Ratzinger, who was part of shaping that legacy. He himself was, of course, a different personality from John Paul II, who was an extrovert and who took energy from people. He would enter a room rather tired and he would leave the room energized, especially in encounters with young people. He had people at his daily Mass in the Apostolic Palace and at practically every meal.

He was a great listener—he would listen and listen and listen and, most striking of all, at the end of a conversation, he displayed a form of humor that was basically ironic. He would make fun of himself, so he was free to make fun of you! There was therefore, on the part of the cardinals, a desire that John Paul's legacy be continued. Benedict was elected and did a remarkable job, contributing again to the magisterium. What he wrote will be read hundreds of years from now, perhaps in the second lesson of the Breviary (office of readings). But when he resigned there was a clear sense among the cardinals that we needed somebody not so much to continue now but to change. There was a concern to change so that ecclesiastical governance would be more assured, particularly through the reform of the Curia. We knew that things weren't working well, because when the Curia doesn't work well, then we can't work well—as bishops of local churches. It doesn't mesh the way it should. And the curial cardinals were the most critical of the way the Curia was operating. So the governance issue was before us very clearly and that concern is what I and others went with to Rome as we prepared to elect a successor to Pope Benedict XVI.

Also in my own mind, in an interview with the *New York Times* at the time, I said there are two things to look for: someone who knows how to govern and someone who has a heart for the poor because the poor are the first in the kingdom of heaven, and we all enter the kingdom of God holding the hands of poor people, or we won't get there at all. We also wanted someone who was young enough to have the strength to go forward. That is why, in the beginning of the discussion, Cardinal Bergoglio was not often mentioned as a candidate. We were looking for somebody younger who would have the good health to pick up the work that had slowed somewhat in the later years of Pope Benedict. Pope Benedict's health now seems much improved. I remember talking to Archbishop Gänswein, his secretary, about a week after Benedict had resigned and gone to Castel Gandolfo. I asked the archbishop how Pope Benedict was doing and he said, if I remember correctly, "Mostly he sleeps." People who have seen him recently (I haven't) have said that he is himself again. Obviously he was worn out.

Before the conclave begins, as you know, there are two weeks when all the cardinals, the electors (under eighty) and those who are over eighty get together every morning in the Synod Hall in the Paul VI Auditorium and converse. One is free to speak about anything one wants to speak about. Mostly, they talk about issues facing the Church or about the conditions of their local church or about what kind of pope we should have. You get to speak for a number of minutes. There's no exact order to the give-and-take. You speak in the order in which you have asked to speak. So you don't have someone speaking to what somebody just said before. It's an odd conversation. The synods have that drawback as well. Nonetheless, everybody gets to speak if he wants to, and most do. In those conversations in the mornings people begin to define what the Church needs but also, to some extent, they define themselves. The cardinals come from around the world, and we get to know each other sometimes at meetings, sometimes in other ways as well; we're all acquainted but not necessarily friends or deeply cognizant of each other. Those conversations are interesting and in them, as has been reported, the present pope gave a very moving intervention about not being a self-referential Church, that is, a Church that speaks more about the Church herself than about Christ, her Lord. So that brought Cardinal Bergoglio back to the forefront of people's minds and helped identify him to some extent as someone who could be the sort of missionary pope, again, that we felt that we needed.

In the afternoons there are no meetings, but the cardinals meet one another or they don't, as they wish, over coffee or at supper, two or three or four at a time. At that point it is not so much issues that are discussed as candidates. That's when you ask about people. You know Cardinal so-and-so; I don't. What do you think of him? Could he be pope? That's all part of the discernment. In the evening, you are pretty much to yourself and that's when you bring what you've learned to your prayer before the Lord. The conclave is to be an exercise in discernment, which means you have to be free to discern what God wants and not what your own interests might lead you to choose. It is very difficult, as you know if you've been involved in those processes of discernment, to achieve the inner freedom necessary to say, "Well, I'm not going to vote for any motive except: Is he the best candidate that I can think of to fill the papal office?" Not: Is he my friend? Not: Does he know my language? Not: Is he going to be understanding of my own situation? Nothing except: Who can be the universal pastor of the Catholic Church? It's the only motive that is morally correct as you go into the conclave. All that takes some time to achieve, because we all come with our own good interests—the interests of our people and other interests, perhaps, if they are not sinful.

To examine oneself in that way takes some time, and it also brings into question the freedom of the one being considered. That is, if I have to be entirely free in order to vote for someone who will be the pope, then I have to ask if the candidate is free to accept the office and to exercise it well. There are extrinsic concerns that might hinder a very fine candidate from being effective as pope. What country does he come from? What is his family like? What is he going to bring? Those extrinsic concerns (extrinsic to the person) have to be considered because they do influence people's understanding of who the pope is and therefore what the office can do. The conclave is an exercise of freedom and discernment, as it is supposed to be. Am I free of any interest except what I am there for, and is the person I'm thinking about free to exercise the office?

In the conclave itself, there are no discussions. People seem to think that, because there is an election, the conclave is a kind of political gathering, with people getting up and saying, "Vote for so-and-so." There's none of that at all. It's a liturgy; you're in liturgical dress, the red robes of the cardinal at Mass. You pray in Latin, and you're instructed in Italian, and then you vote. You pray and you vote, you pray and you vote. You can speak quietly to the people next to you, if you like, but the people next to you are always the same people because you are seated in order of precedence. I am next to the archbishop of Mexico City, Cardinal Rivera, and next to him is the archbishop of Vienna, Cardinal Schönborn. On my right used to be the archbishop of Lviv of the Latins until he died. He was a philosopher, and we used to speak in French, and his place has been taken by Cardinal Grocholewski, who is the prefect of the Congregation for Education.

You can talk, and you do, but basically you vote and you pray, because it takes a long time to vote. (If you want to see what the voting process is, you can look it up on the Vatican website.) It's a long process. You take an oath, which is very solemn, not to have any motive in voting for someone except who is best suited for the office, and that concern dominates the entire proceeding. The election takes place, as you know, in the Sistine Chapel, with the creation of the world on the ceiling by the young Michelangelo and the end of the world on the wall by the old Michelangelo. You are situated in the history of the salvation of the world making a very important choice, knowing that you have to answer to Christ who is your judge.

Because the conclave was an exercise in discernment, I firmly believe that we have the pope that the Holy Spirit wants us to have. The Spirit is a Spirit of surprises. There was no surprise by the time Cardinal Bergoglio was elected, but the name the Spirit chose was a surprise. From the very beginning, therefore, he has shown a certain freedom that is attractive. He's in a tradition-bound office, and the traditions unite us to Christ—there's a reason for them—yet within them he's free, and I think that is, probably more than anything else, what has captured the imagination of the world. You don't expect a man in that office to be as free as this pope is. He has been set free by Christ. His is not a freedom gained by controlling anything; it is a freedom that is a pure gift. He showed the freedom, first of all, by his choice of a name. Francis is not a papal name; it's not a Roman name. And the name is a program, as we know now, as he himself said when he took it. From the beginning, he's shown a certain freedom as a disciple of the Lord, to fulfill the obligations of the papal office but do it in such a way that he does it with a style that is substance.

He is somebody who has had long experience in governing, both as a religious superior and as a bishop. He knows how to govern, and he certainly has a great heart for the poor. What was a surprise to me was the populist approach to his ministry, because that wasn't evident in Buenos Aires.

I'm told he was a rather reserved figure at times, though well respected and certainly concerned about the poor; but he didn't speak to the press, didn't do anything publicly that would indicate he was going to reach around or over the heads of those who are in charge generally in order to appeal directly to the people themselves and adopt the kind of populist approach to ministry that we now have grown to appreciate. That was a surprise; and it has proven to be a good way to solidify his office popularly so that he is then free to make the structural changes that will have to be made.

The sources of his ministry are not so much of a surprise. There's his own spirituality, which is Ignatian, and therefore it gives a larger place to subjectivity than would be the case with other schools of spirituality. There is a use of images for a man who is not an accomplished linguist. He knows how to read all the languages—he's well educated—but he has never had to speak them. He speaks Argentinian Spanish and Italian, and he's learning to speak some English now, but he speaks effectively through gestures that are universal.

In his homilies you can see, too, the way in which he relies upon images rather than concepts. They are always images of encounter, particularly an encounter first of all with Christ but also with those whom Christ most loved, that is, with people at the periphery. As he says, "Go to the frontier, go to the periphery. There you will meet Christ in the face of the poor, and that encounter with the person is where you start." After that, who is Jesus Christ? Doctrine tells you that. How should we be his friend? Moral theology tells you that. But you don't start with ideas. You don't start with rules. You start with relationships in the encounter. The images that have so moved the world are universal, and they speak better than any words possibly could.

Also, his ministry is primarily concerned to make conscious to us the perpetual presence of God's mercy. He made reference to John Paul II's institution of the Divine Mercy devotion and also to his encyclical *Dives in misericordia*. There, John Paul II describes mercy as similar to what I have called "love which is eager to forgive." You start always with forgiveness. You start always with mercy, no matter whom you are talking to or in what circumstance you find yourself. That too comes out of his spirituality. As you know, when he was seventeen years old, he went to make his confession. Instead of just going through a list of sins and receiving absolution, he said, "Somebody welcomed me. There was a presence; there was someone waiting for me." And that so touched him that he remains thoroughly convinced that God is always waiting for us. We can count on his mercy always.

It is, of course, one thing to count on God's mercy because you are asking for forgiveness and, if God has forgiven you, "Who am I to judge?" It's another thing to not ask for forgiveness but rather to demand approval for what you do, and that is not what the pope is concerned about. He's not saying we should approve sinners—at least not their sin—because nobody can judge anything. He's saying that when someone is conscious of sin and asks for forgiveness, then you leave the judgment to God. It's a very different approach: asking for forgiveness or demanding approval. There can be misunderstandings, as there have been, and there are certain dangers in an image-prone ministry. Expectations that are raised by it—because images can be interpreted in different ways—will not be met at a certain point, and when that happens there could be some disillusionment and some difficulties as the Church goes on.

Nonetheless, it is very clear that the experience of God's mercy—the use of images and his own spirituality from the Ignatian exercises—are where he is coming from, along with the Aparecida document, which I know you've discussed, too, where the Church is presented as a Church of missionary disciples, unlike the way the Church is often looked at as a service provider. Sometimes the services are sacraments, and sometimes they are the works of mercy: education, health care, etc. The Church as a philanthropic organization for providing social services can distract from the Church's mission. The pope is interested in encountering people. If you can use the social services in order to encounter people and come to know them by name and know their faces, that's the personal approach that leads to Christ. The danger is that the Church allows herself to become an NGO. Pope Francis wants a Church of missionary disciples, and that is a challenge to us here in a highly institutionalized Church. We've created our institutions precisely because we wanted to be ourselves in a hostile social environment a hundred years ago, which is becoming more hostile again. But we have to ask, to what extent have we lost ourselves in ministry and forgotten mission? In other words, we define ourselves by what we do rather than why we do it, its purpose, which is the mission of the Church: to introduce the world to its Savior until he returns again in glory.

One last point. In the Aparecida document, the Church is a community of missionary disciples in the world. But the world is contingent; the world passes away. That too, I think, is part of the pope's consciousness. I was quite surprised when he made reference more than once to (Msgr.) Robert Hugh Benson's book *Lord of the World*. I read that book when I was in high school. It was written in 1907. It foresees air travel and all kinds of modern developments, but it is a portrayal of the end of the world, when a very charismatic American senator becomes "Lord of the World" and turns out to be the Antichrist. Since the world is contingent, we shouldn't get so preoccupied by it that we forget that it is the Church's mission that is primary. The mission defines creation rather than the world defining the Church. As from a field hospital, the papal office brings this truth to a wounded world.

Pope Francis has picked up the new evangelization that was first proclaimed by the Council itself, and then described more clearly by John Paul II and continued by Benedict XVI. Pope Francis has picked that up, but with the emphases of his own spirituality and personal insight. We'll see how his approach works itself out in the context of the Synod for the Family. That will be the first test of how much impact he will have on a world that has defined families in a way that is antithetical to divine revelation. I thank you for your attention.

2

Foot Washing

Reflections on the Fourth Gospel and the Exemplary Leadership of Pope Francis

BARBARA E. REID, OP

Pope Francis had only been in office twelve days when he chose to go to a juvenile detention center on Holy Thursday, where he washed the feet of twelve youths. In a video released by the Vatican, Pope Francis was shown kneeling on the stone floor, washing, then kissing the feet of teens who were black, white, male, and female, including Orthodox Christians and two Muslim women. If the gesture itself were not clear enough, he explained, "This is a symbol, it is a sign. Washing your feet means I am at your service . . . Help one another. This is what Jesus teaches us. This is what I do. And I do it with my heart."[1]

In the almost eleven months since Cardinal Jorge Bergoglio became pope, his leadership style has captured the attention of people from every walk of life the world over. *Time* magazine named him person of the year for 2013.[2] Next he appeared on the cover of *Rolling Stone*—a veritable pop icon![3] When *Vanity Fair Italia* named him Man of the Year, their cover

---

1. Winfield, "Pope Francis Washes Feet of Young Detainees in Ritual."
2. Chua-Eoan and Dias, "Pope Francis, the People's Pope."
3. Binelli, "Pope Francis."

story noted, "His first one hundred days have already placed him in the category of world leaders who make history."[4]

What is it that has made Pope Francis such an impressive leader? And how can we learn from him? Studies in how to lead effectively have become quite an industry in recent years. People like Margaret Wheatley have helped us understand how new models of leadership are needed that are attuned to the rhythms of the cosmos.[5] Leadership theorists are studying quantum physics, the science of self-organizing systems, and chaos theory, showing that models of command and control no longer serve. Peter Block has articulated how leaders can bring about collective transformation by focusing on possibility, generosity, and gifts, rather than problem-solving, fear, and retribution.[6] Ron Heifetz has elaborated ways in which adaptive leadership values diversity over central management and risks experimentation in the face of changing realities.[7] For Donna Markham, the key is "spiritlinking"—the work of building circles of friends and fostering networks of human compassion "through which new ideas are born and new ways of responding to the mission take form and find expression."[8] Peter Senge, Otto Scharmer, and other proponents of Theory U challenge leaders to begin not with predetermined outcomes and a strategic plan for achieving them but with deep nondefensive listening, allowing the group's inner knowing to emerge and then co-creating with members the actions and structures to move to the preferred future.[9]

All of these leadership theorists have great wisdom to offer, and perhaps Pope Francis has studied them. But what seems to me the most apparent influence on our current pontiff is his relationship with Jesus and the model of his leadership as portrayed in the Gospel. I invite you to examine with me the pattern of leadership exemplified by Jesus in the foot-washing scene in the Gospel of John, and then we will reflect on how Pope Francis follows this model, one that is possible for all of us to emulate.

---

4. Hafiz, "Pope Francis Named Man of the Year."
5. Wheatley, *Leadership and the New Science.*
6. Block, *Community.*
7. Heifetz et al., *Practice of Adaptive Leadership.*
8. Markham, *Spiritlinking Leadership.*
9. Senge et al., *Presence.*

Foot Washing (John 13:1–20): An Acted Parable

A. Beyond Humble Service and Hospitality

Much has been written about the meaning of Jesus's washing of his disciples' feet. All agree that it is an act that is rich in symbolic meaning. But not all agree on what that meaning is. Some scholars see the foot washing as an example of humble service, of Jesus "lowering" himself to perform a service that pertained to slaves. It is a reversal of roles, the master taking on the role of servant. Others have advanced the idea that the foot washing is an act of hospitality, even of eschatological hospitality; that is, it is a symbolic welcoming of the disciples into the place where Jesus is going, the house of the Father.[10] There is validity to these and other interpretations. I would argue, however, that they do not go far enough in plumbing the depths of the symbolic meaning.

B. A Metaphor for Jesus's Death: Appointing His Life for His Friends

I would advance that the foot washing is an acted out parable, a prophetic act that helps us interpret Jesus's death as the consequence of the way he has appointed his life for his friends.[11] It is one of a whole series of metaphors for Jesus's death in the Fourth Gospel, along with the uplifting of the bronze serpent (3:14–16), the giving of his flesh for the life of the world (6:51), the outpouring of water at Tabernacles (7:37–39), the good shepherd who lays down his life for his sheep (10:11), and the seed that must die before it can bring forth fruit (12:24).[12]

The opening verse of John 13 makes it clear that the foot washing is not a simple gesture of humility, nor a singular act, but symbolizes the way in which Jesus has embodied God's love throughout his earthly sojourn, a costly love that culminates in his laying down his life for his own. "Having loved his own who were in the world, he loved them to the end [*eis telos*]." The link to Jesus's death is made with the phrase *eis telos*, which has two nuances: he loved them "completely" and he loved them "to the end." The word *telos* points ahead and creates an inclusio—one of the Fourth

---

10. Hultgren, "Johannine Footwashing," 539–46.
11. In what follows, I rely heavily on Schneiders, "Community of Friends," 184–201.
12. Dunn, "Washing of the Disciples' Feet," 249.

Evangelist's favorite literary techniques—with John 19:30, the crucifixion scene, where Jesus's final word is *tetelestai*, "it is finished," a word that has the same root as *telos*.

John 13:1 also emphasizes that what Jesus is doing is entirely motivated by love. At the center of this action that symbolizes his life and death is love, not atonement for sin. This is also brought to the fore in the crucifixion scene, to which we will return shortly.

C. His Own

Verse 1 also calls attention to "his own" (*tous idíous*) as the object of Jesus's love. This expression occurs also in the Prologue, which says in verse 11, "He came to his own, but his own did not accept him" (1:11), and again in chapter 10, where the good shepherd "calls his own sheep by name and leads them out. When he has brought out all his own, he goes ahead of them, and the sheep follow him" (10:3–4). Jesus's "own" are most often called "disciples" (*mathētai*) in the Fouth Gospel. The term occurs seventy-eight times and refers to all those who are taught by Jesus and who believe in him. In verse 5, Jesus washes the feet of the disciples. In this Gospel, there is no story of the call of the Twelve, or sending of the Twelve, as in the Synoptic Gospels. References to the Twelve occur in only three verses: twice at the end of the account of the feeding of the five thousand, where "Jesus said to the twelve, 'Do you also wish to go away?'" (6:67), and then "Did I not choose you, the twelve . . . ?" (6:70) The third instance is in the resurrection appearance in 20:24, where Thomas is identified as one of the Twelve. The Twelve play no real role in the Fourth Gospel. Neither is there reference to the Twelve being apostles, as in the Gospel of Luke. The only time the word *apostolos* occurs in the Fourth Gospel is in 13:16, to which I will return.

The notion that there were only twelve at the Last Supper and that they were all male cannot be sustained by the account in the Fourth Gospel, the only Gospel that gives us this story. The only characters named in the account besides Jesus are Peter and Judas. The Beloved Disciple, who reclines on Jesus's bosom (13:23), is never named in the Gospel. In the narrative, this character symbolizes all disciples, loved by Jesus and loving him in return. Each of Jesus's followers can insert himself or herself in the scene. The intimacy between beloved disciples and Jesus (ἐν τῷ κόλπῳ τοῦ Ἰησοῦ) is expressed in the very same language as the intimacy between the Son and the Father, in the Prologue (v. 18): "the only Son, who is in the bosom of the Father" (NRSV, εἰς τὸν κόλπον τοῦ πατρὸς).[13]

D. Timing: The "Hour"

The opening verse (13:1) sets the stage for a new moment: "Jesus knew that the hour had come for him to depart from this world and go to the Father." In the first half of the Gospel, there are frequent references to the coming "hour," which has not yet come.[14] The "hour" is shorthand for Jesus's passion, death, resurrection, ascension, glorification, and giving of the Spirit, which is all one moment in this Gospel.

One of the critical skills for a leader is to discern the proper timing for prophetic action. When does one need to retreat from the conflictual situation and wait for the propitious moment to act? How does one know whether it is the moment to stay the course and face possible deadly consequences? In John 11 we see Jesus weighing the decision whether or not to go to Jerusalem. His opponents have been trying to stone him (8:59; 10:31) or arrest him (10:39), and the disciples remind Jesus of that (11:8). After delaying for two days, Jesus decides to go to his friend Lazarus in Judea. Thomas rightly voices the danger: "Let us also go that we may die with him" (11:16). And, indeed, following the raising of Lazarus, the Jewish leaders plan to put Jesus to death (11:53).

A glimpse into how Jesus came to know the right time can be seen at the end of chapter 10. At the conclusion of a verbal duel with his opponents, after which they tried to arrest him, John 10:40 says that Jesus "went away again across the Jordan to the place where John had been baptizing earlier, and he remained there." Jesus returns to the place where he began to be mentored by John and where he first joined in the baptizing ministry (John 3:26). In the desert space that fosters contemplative oneness with the One who sent him, he is able to touch the deepest core of who he is and what his love and God's love of his friends asks of him. Although the Fourth Gospel does not relate the death of John the Baptist, we may surmise that at this point John has been executed. Jesus sees the handwriting on the wall—that John's fate also awaits him.

---

13. Other translations mask this important parallel, translating 1:18 as "close to the Father's heart" (NAB); "at the Father's side" (NJB).

14. John 2:4; 4:21, 23; 5:25, 28–29; 7:30; 8:20; 16:2, 25, 32.

E. Passover Symbolism (13:1)

The opening verse also calls attention to the imminent feast of Passover. This is highly significant, signaling that the life and death of Jesus is the new liberation for God's people from all that holds them bound. The Johannine chronology of the passion is different from that of the Synoptics. The Last Supper in the Fourth Gospel is not a Passover meal. At the start of the Gospel, John the Baptist identifies Jesus as "the Lamb of God who takes away the sin of the world" (1:29, 36). Thus, Jesus dies at the moment that the Passover lambs for the feast are being slaughtered in the temple. Following his death, his legs are not broken (John 19:33), just as no bone of the Passover lamb may be broken (Exod 12:46). The Passover lamb is a sign of liberation, not of sacrificial atonement. The manner in which sins are taken away is not through one act of expiatory death but through a life spent in extending divine mercy and forgiveness to all, with a love that liberates. Moreover, the liberator himself is completely free, as he stresses in the good shepherd discourse: "I lay down my life . . . No one takes it from me; I lay it down of my own free will, and as I have power to lay it down, so I have power to take it up again" (10:17–18).

F. John 13:15—"Example" (*hypodeigma*)

Other keys to understanding the model of leadership Jesus offers us are in vv. 12–20, where Jesus explains to the disciples what he has done for them. In v. 15 he says, "I have given you an example [*hypodeigma*], that you also should do as I have done for you." The word *hypodeigma*, "example" or "model," appears a number of times in the Septuagint in contexts where it exhorts the faithful to mark an exemplary death.[15] For instance, in 2 Maccabees 6:18–31, when Eleazar was being forced to eat pork, he chose "death with honor rather than life with pollution" (6:19). He says, "by bravely giving up my life I . . . leave to the young a noble example [*hypodeigma*] of how to die a good death willingly and nobly for the revered and holy laws" (6:27–28). Similar examples can be found in 4 Maccabees 17:22–23 and Sirach 44:16. Just so, Jesus's exemplary leadership involves a willingness to die for those he loves.

---

15. Culpepper, "Johannine *Hypodeigma*," 142.

G. John 13:16—"Servant" (*doulos*) and "Messenger" (*apostolos*)

As Jesus continues to explain the foot washing, he says, "a servant [*doulos*] is not greater than the master, nor is a messenger [*apostolos*] greater than the one who sent him" (John 13:16). In the first half of the verse, Jesus calls attention to leadership as service. As Sandra Schneiders has elaborated,[16] what he has enacted during his lifetime, and crystallized in his symbolic action of foot washing, is a model of service based on friendship. This differs significantly from other models of service. One type of service is that which is owed to another who is in a superior position, as in service rendered by a slave to a master. Another kind is service that someone who has an ability renders to another in need—for example, parents for their children, or teachers for their students. In both these types there is an inequality of status and a certain level of obligation. The type of service Jesus models, by contrast, is that of friend to friend. In John 15 Jesus speaks explicitly to those gathered at this final supper as his friends. He says, "No one has greater love than this, to lay down one's life for one's friends" (15:13). And then, "You are my friends if you do what I command you" (15:14). What he has commanded is, "Just as I have loved you, you also should love one another" (13:34). So, the love of friends asks for freely given service to one another, even to the point of willingness to lay down one's life for the friend. Not only does Jesus do this for his friends, but he gives the example for all his friends to do likewise.

It is important to note that in the model of service of friend to friend, the service is not obligatory but is freely chosen and evokes a response in kind from the other. It is not, however, simply a reciprocal service among a closed circle of friends but one that reaches out to draw in other people, even those not among one's own kind. Jesus exemplifies this in John 4, when he crosses into Samaritan territory to turn enmity between his people and theirs into friendship. Although the term is not used of her in the text, the woman Jesus meets at the well, who brings her townspeople to believe in him as "Savior of the world" (4:42), is the one who embodies what it is to be an apostle in this Gospel. The word *apostolos*, "one sent," appears for the first time in 13:16, when Jesus says that the "messenger," *apostolos*, is not greater than the One who sends. The theme of sending culminates in John 20:21, where the fearful disciples are gathered behind closed doors and the

---

16. Schneiders, "Community of Friends," 192–95.

risen Christ appears in their midst, breathes the Spirit upon them, and says, "As the Father has sent me, so I send you."

One other important observation about the model of service among friends is that the love offered is not always reciprocated. Nonetheless, Jesus does not skip over the one who is about to deny he ever knew him, nor the one who is about to hand him over to those who want him dead. He washes the feet of all.

Note, too, that in this model of service of friend toward friend there is no inequality of status. As Aristotle asserted, friendship levels the distinctions between unequal partners.[17] So those who would see Jesus's washing of the disciples' feet as a "lowering" of himself are not quite on target with the way the Johannine community of friends is depicted. At the very beginning of this Gospel, the Prologue speaks of how "the Word became flesh and dwelt among us" (1:14), that is, the Incarnate Word takes on the same status as humankind. We then see how the Johannine Jesus is intent on creating a community of disciples in which all know themselves as equally beloved and become empowered to be apostles of that love. Note that there is no hierarchy of relationship among the disciples in this Gospel. There are none who are singled out and given the keys to the kingdom of heaven (as in Matt 16:19). There is no inner circle of twelve in this Gospel, no calling of the Twelve, nor sending of the Twelve.[18] There are not three singled out for special relationship with Jesus, such as Peter, James, and John in the Synoptic Gospels.[19] There is the Beloved Disciple, who remains anonymous throughout. Any reader of the Gospel can insert himself or herself into the place of the one who is most loved, who rests his or her head upon Jesus's breast at the Last Supper (13:23), who stands in witness at the foot of the cross (19:26), and who is the first to believe at the empty tomb (20:8). All disciples are the most beloved and all are friends of equal status.

Having equal status does not mean, however, that they are without difference. In the community of beloved disciples, there are differences, but those differences do not matter when it comes to one's standing in the community. It is as Paul put it in his letter to the Galatians: "There is no longer Jew or Greek, there is no longer slave or free, there is no longer male and female, for all are one in Christ Jesus" (3:28).

---

17 Aristotle, *Nicomachean Ethics* VIII.xi.7. See Ringe, *Wisdom's Friends*, 70.

18. The only references to the Twelve occur in John 6:67, 70, 71; 20:24. The last two references simply identify Judas and Thomas as "one of the twelve."

19. Mark 1:19, 29; 5:37; 9:2; 13:3; 14:33 and parallels.

Another important aspect of the love of friends is that this is a freely chosen relationship. As Sallie McFague observes, friendship is the freest of all human relationships.[20] "It is not bound by biological ties or by duties, nor by function or office."[21] Service that friends render to friends is freely given, never coerced, leaving the recipient free to respond or not. It is ironic that in John 13:16 Jesus uses the word *doulos*, literally "slave," when he says "a servant [*doulos*] is not greater than the master." Servitude or enforced servility is completely antithetical to the kind of relationship Jesus models for disciples.

Later, in the Final Discourse, Jesus envisions an end to servitude in John 15:15, when he says, "I do not call you servants [*doulous*] any longer, because the servant [*doulos*] does not know what the master is doing; but I have called you friends, because I have made known to you everything that I have heard from my Father." In order to arrive at equality in the community of disciples, there must be a two-pronged movement. Those who have been trapped in systems of servility and submission must embrace a theology of empowerment, while those who have power, privilege, and status must embrace a theology of relinquishment.[22]

Such an overturning of patterns of relating based on domination and subordination is not accomplished without a struggle. In the foot-washing scene, Peter objects vigorously to what Jesus is doing: "By no means [*ou mē* is an emphatic negative] will you wash my feet!" (13:8). As Sandra Schneiders observes, "In some way, Peter grasped that complicity in this act involved acceptance of a radical reinterpretation of his own life-world, a genuine conversion of some kind, which he was not prepared to undergo."[23] This is the Johannine equivalent to the firm rejection by Peter of Jesus's prediction of the passion in the synoptic tradition (Mark 8:32–33 and parallels). It is not only Jesus's death or even his manner of execution that Peter protests, but the manner of life that Jesus models that leads to that death.

H. John 13:19—"That You May Believe That I AM"

At the conclusion of Jesus's explanation of the foot washing, he says, "I tell you this now, so that when it does occur, you may believe that I AM" (John

20. McFague, *Models of God*, 159.
21. Ford, *Redeemer—Friend and Mother*, 73.
22. Schüssler Fiorenza, "'Waiting at Table,'" 84–94.
23. Schneiders, "Community of Friends," 191.

13:19). In using the formulation *egō eimi*, "I AM," Jesus's identifies himself with the divine name revealed to Moses (Exod 3:14). In appropriating the title "I AM" to himself, Jesus affirms that he is the incarnation of the same liberating God.

There are also a number of instances in the Fourth Gospel in which Jesus uses *egō eimi* with a predicate: "I am the Bread of Life" (6:35, 48); "I am the Light of the world" (8:12; 9:5); "I am the gate to the sheepfold" (10:7, 9); "I am the good shepherd" (10:11); "I am the Way, the Truth, and the Life" (14:6); and "I am the true vine" (15:1). Each of these terms except "good shepherd" is also associated with Woman Wisdom, who also speaks as "I AM" in many instances in the books of Proverbs, Sirach, and Wisdom.[24] In addition, there are strong parallels between what is said of the *Logos* in the Prologue of the Fourth Gospel and what is said of Woman Wisdom in Job 28; Proverbs 1-9; Baruch 3:9—4:4; Sirach 1; 4:11-19; 6:18-31; 14:20-15; and Wisdom 6-10. Both existed with God from the beginning, both are an emanation of the glory of God, both descend from heaven to dwell with humans and will return to heaven, both light the path for humans and teach them the things from above, leading them to life and immortality. As I AM, Jesus is the incarnation of the divine, which can be imaged both as female and male. Both he himself and his community of friends transcend gender; both females and males are his beloved friends, both females and males embody his model of leadership.

Francis the Foot Washer

Having examined the symbolism of the foot-washing scene in John's Gospel, I would like to turn now to Francis the foot washer and the ways in which he is leading us to follow Christ's model. First, like Jesus, Pope Francis understands the power of symbolic action. As Thomas Reese, former editor of *America* magazine, commented when asked whether the change in leadership with Pope Francis was more a question of style over substance, "We are a church of symbols. That's what we call the sacraments: symbols that give us grace. These things really matter. So Francis is already changing the church in real ways through his words and symbolic gestures."[25]

---

24. Ringe, *Wisdom's Friends*, 61. See Prov 3:17, 18; 8:7, 32, 34, 35, 38; Sir 6:26; 24:17, 19, 21; Wis 6:22; 7:26; 18:34.

25. Spadaro, "A Big Heart Open to God."

Humility

I have argued that Jesus's washing of his disciples' feet was more than an act of humility, but for those who emulate Jesus's style of leadership, the virtue of humility is essential. In one symbolic gesture after another, Pope Francis's humility shines through. In the very first public moment of his papacy, Pope Francis humbly asked for the blessing of the people assembled. He dispensed with tradition on the day he was elected and refused the *mozzetta*, the red cape, and kept his own simple iron pectoral cross. He has chosen to live in a modest two-bedroom apartment in the Casa Santa Marta rather than the Apostolic Palace. He wears sensible dark-colored loafers instead of fancy red ones. He prefers to ride around town in a used Ford Focus rather than a chauffeured Mercedes limo. He makes his own phone calls, pays his own bills, carries his own briefcase. As Rex Huppke commented in the *Chicago Tribune*, he is making the "i" in leading nearly invisible.[26]

Love for His Own—Includes All

In the foot washing in John's Gospel, we saw that love for his own was the central force in Jesus's life appointed for his friends. Likewise, Pope Francis's experience of God's steadfast love and endless mercy colors his every word and deed. His apostolic exhortation, *Evangelii gaudium*, opens with an invitation to accept anew God's constant love and boundless mercy. But more than with words, Pope Francis expresses such love in gesture after gesture, especially as he embraces those who are thrust to the margins. For his birthday in December, for example, he invited four homeless people to join him along with household employees at a morning Mass. Last October, when a six-year-old orphan wandered onstage and clung to Pope Francis's leg, the delighted pontiff encouraged the boy to stay with him, over the protests of his aides. In November, he unhesitatingly embraced tightly a man with a severely disfiguring disease whom no one would sit with on the bus. He has had the protective glass covering the pope mobile removed and travels through St. Peter's Square with his windows rolled down, touching hands with everyone he can. He explained, "When you go to see someone you love, are you going to visit them inside a glass box?"

Like Jesus, who sought to befriend all, Pope Francis has reached out widely, even to atheists. In *Evangelii gaudium* he says, "No one should think

26. Huppke, "Lessons in Leadership from Pope Francis."

that this invitation is not meant for him or her, since 'no one is excluded from the joy brought by the Lord'" (para. 3).

He invites us to share his dream of a church that "does not just welcome and receive all by keeping the doors open, but one that finds new roads, that steps outside itself to go to those who have quit or are indifferent. It is a home for all, not a small chapel that can hold only a small group of select people."[27]

Apostoloi

As the Johannine Jesus empowered his disciples to be sent forth as *apostles*, so Pope Francis dreams, as he says in *Evangelii gaudium*, of a "missionary impulse capable of transforming everything, so that the Church's customs, ways of doing things, times and schedules, language and structures can be suitably channeled for the evangelization of today's world rather than for her self-preservation." He hopes to "make ordinary pastoral activity on every level more inclusive and open, to inspire in pastoral workers a constant desire to go forth and in this way to elicit a positive response from all those whom Jesus summons to friendship with himself" (para. 27).

Nonhierarchical Relationships

We saw that within the community of Jesus's friends in the Fourth Gospel, all were equally beloved and there were no hierarchical distinctions. While Pope Francis has inherited a church quite hierarchically structured, he is leading the way in diminishing clerical privilege and in sharing governance. He has formed a group of eight other leaders, cardinals from nearly every continent, who will work with him in important matters of governance. He has set up a commission to advise him on how best to deal with the problem of pedophilia within the Church. He has asked for the input of Catholics the world over in preparation for the fall 2015 Synod on the Family. He told Antonio Spadaro last September in the interview that appeared in *America* magazine that he wants to be thinking with the Church, that dialogue among all the people and bishops and himself is needed, pastors and people together. And in *Evangelii gaudium*, he says, "I am conscious of the need to promote a sound 'decentralization'" (para. 16). "Excessive

---

27. Spadaro, "A Big Heart Open to God."

centralization," he goes on to say, "rather than proving helpful, complicates the Church's life and her missionary outreach" (para. 32).

Many of us hope that Pope Francis's steps toward shared leadership will extend to women in the Church in more significant ways in the future. It is heartening to hear him express the desire "to create still broader opportunities for a more incisive female presence in the Church."[28] It is not yet clear what Pope Francis means by this. Females have been present in the church since its inception; women such as Mary Magdalene, Joanna, and Susanna (Luke 8:3) were among Jesus's first disciples, witnessed his death, were the first to see him resurrected, and to fulfill his commission to proclaim the gospel. Women like Phoebe (Rom 16:1-2) have been deacons and patrons; women like Prisca (Acts 18:1-4, 26; Rom 16:3-5) have been teachers, evangelizers, heads of house churches, traveling missionaries; and women like Junia (Rom 16:7) have been notable among the apostles. There has always been a female presence in the church, but it has been noticeably absent in the arenas of sacramental ministry, leadership and decision-making.

In *Evangelii gaudium*, paragraph 103, Pope Francis says that "the presence of women must be guaranteed in . . . the various settings where important decisions are made, both in the Church and in social structures." If Pope Francis could quietly, with one symbolic gesture, lay to rest the notion that women cannot participate in the foot-washing ritual on Holy Thursday, there is great hope that he will discern the propitious time, "the hour," for other ways to ensure the full flourishing of women's gifts in the Church in every arena.

A Leader a Lifetime in the Making

The style of leadership that Pope Francis has developed is not something that he adopted just as he became pope; it is the fruit of a lifetime of choosing to live by the example set by Jesus. Chris Lowney, a one-time Jesuit seminarian and author of *Pope Francis: Why He Leads the Way He Leads*,[29] calls attention to the lengthy training Jesuits undergo, schooled in self-examination and working among the people they seek to lead. He calls it "dirty-footed leadership" with a focus on understanding other people

---

28. Pope Francis, *Evangelii gaudium*, 103.
29. Lowney, *Pope Francis*.

and their circumstances and putting their needs ahead of one's own.[30] In his interview with Antonio Spadaro, SJ, published in *America* magazine, Pope Francis spoke of how he has learned from previous experience how to become the kind of leader he is today. He spoke regretfully of how, as provincial of his congregation at age thirty-six, he would make decisions abruptly and without consultation, and of how his authoritarian way of making decisions caused serious problems. Later, as archbishop of Buenos Aires, he would meet with the six auxiliary bishops every two weeks, and several times a year with the council of priests. He invited them to ask questions and opened the floor for discussion. This, he said, greatly helped him make the best decisions.

A Contagious Joy

One of the most effective leadership qualities of Pope Francis is his contagious joy and evident freedom. He has accepted a ministry with the heaviest of responsibilities, yet he constantly exudes a radiant joy. His apostolic exhortation, *Evangelii gaudium* (*The Joy of the Gospel*), makes it crystal clear that the source of his joy, available to all, is the personal relationship with Christ, who is the embodiment of God's boundless love and mercy. Like the Johannine Jesus, who tells his disciples at the Last Supper that his impending passion is like birth pangs that will give way to joy, once the new life is brought forth (16:20), Pope Francis's focus is unwaveringly on life to the full for all (John 10:10) and the costly love that such requires. He does not flinch in the face of those who criticize him for denouncing the personal greed and the sinful structures that make so many people poor. Having been freed himself by the Lamb of God who takes away the sin of the world, he is able to lead the church toward liberating action for all who are held bound.

In expounding on the joy of the Gospel, Pope Francis adopts a theology evident in the Gospel of John, which stresses the centrality of divine love, not atonement for sin. In his exhortation at the end of the Way of the Cross at World Youth Day in Rio de Janeiro in July 2013, he made this most explicit. He exhorted the young people, "The cross of Christ is an invitation for us to fall in love with him and to then reach out and help our neighbors ... The cross gives us an assurance of the unshakable love which God has for us ... a love so great that it enters into our sin and forgives it, enters into

---

30. As described by Rex Huppke, "Lessons in Leadership from Pope Francis."

our suffering and gives us the strength to bear it. It is a love which enters into death to conquer it and to save us . . . Jesus' cross contains 'all the love of God, his immeasurable mercy.'"[31]

How much more effective is a leader who lives out of a theology of love and mercy than preachers who focus on the immensity of human sinfulness and the great debt that had to be paid to God! A leader whose dominant image is that of a punishing God who demands reparation may attract a following of those who respond out of guilt or fear, but such a leader rarely succeeds in winning hearts and minds. In *Evangelii gaudium*, Pope Francis says, "A person who is not convinced, enthusiastic, certain and in love, will convince nobody" (para. 266).

Conclusion

Pope Francis is not perfect in his emulation of Jesus, the foot washer. When asked who is Jorge Mario Bergoglio, his reply was, "A sinner." But he immediately added, "I am a sinner whom the Lord has looked upon."[32] Pope Francis is a leader who has been a lifetime in the making and who is still learning, praying, and listening, while inspiring authentic renewal in the Church. It is undeniable that Pope Francis's manner of leading is having a great impact not only on Catholics but on people of all faiths, and even those of no faith. He is not the product of a leadership training program that promises to make you an effective leader after one or two workshops or through reading a book with seven fail-safe steps. Living the joy of the Gospel is a very different enterprise than following the seven steps to success through the power of positive thinking. This charismatic leader has spent his life immersed in prayer and service, learning to love from the foot washer Jesus, his friend and guide. He has learned how to make Jesus's friends his own, especially those shunted to the margins, and has freely chosen again and again to lay down his life for them. I suspect he would say that the real test of his success as a leader will be not how much admiration he evokes from us but how well we take to heart the example he sets and replicate it in our own manner of leading.

---

31. "Jesus' Cross Invites Us."
32. Spadaro, "A Big Heart Open to God."

3

The Next Step[1]

ABRAHAM SKORKA

During the almost two-thousand-year-long history of relations between Jews and Christians, there have been moments of encounter and deep dialogue, as well as moments of clashes and hatred. Israel Jacob Yuval's book *Two Nations in Your Womb*[2] presents a very well-documented study about the complex relationships between Jews and Christians in medieval Europe, and Edward H. Flannery's famous *The Anguish of the Jews*[3] provides a meticulous history of twenty-three centuries of anti-Semitism, in which Christianity played an important role.

The very survival of the Jewish people presented a challenge to Christian theology. The killers of God's son were still alive, continuing to deny the truth of their faith. The Jews were considered as a *deicidal* people, and as a cursed people they deserved humiliating treatment. European cities like Paris (1240), Barcelona (1263), Tortosa (1413–14), and others have held during their history infamous and dreadful theological disputes between

---

1. Rabbi Skorka originally wrote this text for DePaul University's 2014 conference, "New World Pope," and later, on June 28, 2015, used part of it as a keynote address in Rome for the opening of the International Council of Christians and Jews (ICCJ) conference, "The 50th Anniversary of *Nostra Aetate*: The Past, Present, and Future of the Christian-Jewish Relationship." That 2015 address, titled *"Nostra Aetate*, Past and Future," is accessible online at http://iccj.org/redaktion/upload_pdf/201510021330180. OS_ASkorka_engl.pdf. It is referenced here with the ICCJ's permission.

2. Yuval, *Two Nations*.

3. Flannery, *Anguish of the Jews*.

Jewish and Catholic sages. The common roots in the prophetic words were sanctified by both sides, but their interpretation diverged from one another.

Even in the twentieth century we can find modern "disputations," such as the one carried on as a result of the publications of Adolf von Harnack's classic "The Essence of Christianity" and Leo Baeck's reply to it, *The Essence of Judaism*.[4]

However, the Shoah perpetrated in the heart of Christian Europe clearly demonstrated the futility of vain disputations. The Nazi regime destroyed once and for all the illusion of what Baeck had called "the romantic dimension of religion," which, in contrast to the classical character of the Jewish religion, Christianity had internalized as an essential aspect of its religiosity.[5] The Shoah demanded an answer from Christianity. European culture, in which the Christian component is so important and vital, was bankrupt. The atrocities committed against the Jewish population in the territories under Nazi administration, with the collaboration of many members of the different European peoples, called for much more than mere justice; it called for a deep and critical analysis of the roots of European culture. And the uniqueness of this horrible drama in human history called for a conscientious reaction from the different European churches.

Pope Pius XII passed away on October 9, 1958, and until now there is no registered document under his authorship regarding the Shoah and the theological problem raised. Only his successor, Pope John XXIII, who did so much to rescue Jews during the Second World War, accepted the unavoidable challenge.

On October 11, 1962, after two years of preparations, the Second Vatican Council opened its sessions. On October 28, 1965, the declaration *Nostra aetate* was approved by 2,221 votes in favor and 88 against. Pope Paul VI promulgated solemnly the document.

There are three main affirmations of the document. First: the Jewish people are still beloved by God. Second: one cannot ascribe the death of Jesus even to the entire Jewish population of his time, much less to any of their descendants. Even the infamous word *deicide* does not appear in the text, for theological reasons;[6] the prohibition of blaming the Jews as

---

4. Harnack, *Das Wesen des Christentums*, translated into English as *What Is Christianity?*; Baeck, *The Essence of Judaism*.

5. Baeck, *Judaism and Christianity*, 189–292.

6. Mejía, *Una presencia en el Concilio*, 256–57.

the killers of God becomes explicit. And, third: an explicit condemnation against all kinds of anti-Semitic expressions or teachings.

The declaration was originally intended to address the relationships between the Catholic Church and the Jews; only later on were paragraphs added that related to Islam and other religions. John XXIII was the one who took the initiative for such a declaration and entrusted its first rendition to Cardinal Augustin Bea,[7] who maintained a fruitful dialogue with Rabbi Abraham Joshua Heschel on the issue. *Nostra aetate* fulfills the requirements presented by Rabbi Heschel in a famous memorandum[8] to Cardinal Bea on May 22, 1962.

On December 1, 1974, Johannes Cardinal Willebrands and Pierre-Marie de Contenson, OP, president and secretary respectively of the Vatican Commission for Religious Relations with the Jews, signed the document "Guidelines and Suggestions for Implementing the Conciliar Declaration *Nostra Aetate* No. 4." On June 24, 1985, Willebrands as president, Pierre Duprey as vice president, and Jorge Mejía as secretary of the Commission, signed the document named "Notes on the Correct Way to Present the Jews and Judaism in Preaching and Catechesis in the Roman Catholic Church." Both documents developed deeply the spirit of *Nostra aetate* No. 4.

Pope John Paul II referred to *Nostra aetate* No. 4 and the abovementioned documents as "milestones in the new Jewish-Catholic relations" in his address at the Great Synagogue of Rome on April 13, 1986. This visit of a pope to a synagogue and the establishment of diplomatic relations between the Holy See and the State of Israel have marked a new horizon for the relations between Jews and the Roman Catholic Church.

Jews were aware of these changes and gestures, and they responded in different ways. For Cardinal Jorge Mejía, one of the important goals in the advancement of the dialogue was the presence and participation in the dialogue of rabbis from the Chief Rabbinate of Israel.

A second document to be considered is the declaration *Dabru Emet*, redacted by a group of Jewish thinkers and signed by 220 intellectuals, which was published in the *New York Times* edition of September 10, 2000. This document tried to pave a way for the development of the relationship, after the steps taken by the Holy See. The document stated eight major points:

---

7. Vatican II, *Documentos del Vaticano II*, 611.
8. Heschel, "On Improving Catholic-Jewish Relations."

1. Jews and Christians worship the same God.
2. Jews and Christians seek authority from the same book.
3. Christians can respect the claim of the Jews to the land of Israel.
4. Jews and Christians together accept the moral principles of the Torah (Pentateuch).
5. Nazism is *not* a Christian phenomenon.
6. The controversy between Jews and Christians will not be settled until God redeems the entire world as promised in Scripture, and no one should be pressed into accepting another's faith.
7. A new relationship between Jews and Christians will not weaken Jewish practice.
8. Jews and Christians must work together for justice and peace.

Several points of the document did not obtain consensus among Jews. One of them is the affirmation that Nazism was not a Christian phenomenon. The text, in that point, literally says,

> *Nazism was not a Christian phenomenon.* Without the long history of Christian anti-Judaism and Christian violence against Jews, Nazi ideology could not have taken hold nor could it have been carried out. Too many Christians participated in, or were sympathetic to, Nazi atrocities against Jews. Other Christians did not protest sufficiently against these atrocities. But Nazism itself was not an inevitable outcome of Christianity. If the Nazi extermination of the Jews had been fully successful, it would have turned its murderous rage more directly to Christians. We recognize with gratitude those Christians who risked or sacrificed their lives to save Jews during the Nazi regime. With that in mind, we encourage the continuation of recent efforts in Christian theology to repudiate unequivocally contempt of Judaism and the Jewish people. We applaud those Christians who reject this teaching of contempt, and we do not blame them for the sins committed by their ancestors.[9]

Cardinal Walter Kasper wrote in 2010,

---

9. The full text of *Dabru Emet* is available online at http://www.jcrelations.net/Dabru+Emet+-+A+Jewish+Statement+on+Christians+and+Christianity.2395.0.html?L=3.

> The history of Jewish-Christian relations is complex and difficult. In addition to some better times, as when bishops took Jews under their protection against pogroms by mobs, there were dark times that have been especially impressed upon the collective Jewish consciousness. The Shoah, the state-sponsored organized murder of approximately six million European Jews, based on primitive racial ideology, is the absolute low point in this history. The Holocaust cannot be attributed to Christianity as such, since it also had clear anti-Christian features. However, centuries-old Christian theological anti-Judaism contributed as well, encouraging a widespread antipathy for Jews, so that ideologically and racially motivated anti-Semitism could prevail in this terrible way, and the resistance against the outrageous inhuman brutality did not achieve that breadth and clarity that one should have expected.[10]

In the words of John T. Pawlikowski,

> The church cannot enter into a fully authentic dialogue with the Jewish community, nor present itself and its teaching as a positive moral voice in contemporary society until it has cleansed its soul of its role in contributing to anti-Semitism.[11]

These kinds of affirmations were accepted by all those who went ahead in the Catholic Church with the letter and spirit of *Nostra aetate*, and they presented an objective and very acceptable point of view for Jews. However, a clear and unambiguous document is still hoped for by Jews from different Christian denominations regarding a critical treatment of all the concepts that paved the way for Christian anti-Semitism, not only those found in the patristic literature but also those that can be found in the New Testament, such as John 8:43–47.

On the one hand, there are Jews[12] who consider Christianity as a "foreign worship"—idolatry—and because of that they have refused to accept the principles outlined in *Dabru Emet*; on the other hand, rabbinical personalities such as HaRav Itzhak Isaac HaLevi Herzog,[13] HaRav Hayim David HaLevi,[14] and others have established on clear *halakhic* grounds that Christianity is a non-idolatrous religion.

10. Kasper, "Foreword," x.
11. Pawlikowski, "Historical Memory and Christian-Jewish Relations," 15.
12. Orthodox Union Institute for Public Affairs, "Statement by Dr. David Berger."
13. Herzog, "Zekhuiot," 169–79.
14. HaLevi, " Darkei Shalom," 71–81.

Dabru Emet elicited criticisms from those of the Jewish people who do not accept an interfaith dialogue. Meir Soloveichik, the great-nephew of the famous Rabbi Joseph Ber Soloveitchik, published a very interesting article titled "How Soloveitchik Saw Interreligious Dialogue" in the April 25, 2003, issue of *Forward*. In it, he explains Rabbi Soloveitchik's reasons for opposing interfaith dialogue. In one paragraph he wrote,

> The Rav's opposition to communal and organizational interfaith dialogue was partly predicated upon the prediction that in our search for common ground—a shared theological language—Jews and Christians might each sacrifice our insistence on the absolute and exclusive truth of our respective faiths, blurring the deep divide between our respective dogmas. In an essay titled "Confrontation," Rabbi Soloveitchik argued that a community's faith is an intimate and often incommunicable affair. Furthermore, a faith by definition insists "that its system of dogmas, doctrines and values is best fitted for the attainment of the ultimate good." In his essay, the Rav warned that sacrificing the exclusive nature of religious truth in the name of dialogue would help neither Jews nor Christians. Any "equalization of dogmatic certitudes, and [the] waiving of eschatological claims, spell the end of the vibrant and great faith experiences of any religious community," he wrote.[15]

Rabbi Soloveitchik's position could be understood only under the superficial meaning of the concept of dialogue, when the dialogue has a merely sympathetic relationship as its target. Real dialogue means much more than that, and Buber's teaching and existential experience could serve as an outstanding example of my own understanding of interfaith dialogue.

The core of Buber's philosophy is the meaning of dialogue, one that could be developed by everyone with himself, with the other, with nature, and with God. He maintained intensive dialogues with Christian theologians such as Rudolf Bultmann, Albert Schweitzer, Rudolf Otto, and Leonhard Ragaz, whose knowledge was essential to his understanding of the New Testament. And it was through that knowledge, which he acquired through a deep dialogue, that he came to affirm that Judaism and Christianity were "two types of faith." In a book entitled precisely *Two Types of Faith*, Buber concludes,

> The faith of Judaism and the faith of Christendom are by nature different in kind, each in conformity with its human basis, and

---

15. Soloveichik, "How Soloveitchik Saw Interreligious Dialogue."

> they will indeed remain different, until mankind is gathered in from the exiles of the "religions" into the Kingship of God. But an Israel striving after the renewal of its faith through the rebirth of the person and a Christianity striving for the renewal of its faith through the rebirth of nations would have something as yet unsaid to say to each other—and help to give to one another—hardly to be conceived at the present time.[16]

Buber stresses a differentiation between Pauline Christianity and Jesus's teachings in the Gospels. The latter he understands in terms of the pure Jewish belief in God—*emunah*—and he argues that a Hellenistic Pauline syncretism transformed that belief into a Greek *pístis*.

Buber proposes in this book a way to develop a deep dialogue with the Christian world. The conditions under which Buber wrote the book are very significant. In his own words,

> I wrote this book in Jerusalem during the days of its so-called siege, or rather in the chaos of destruction which broke out within it. I began it without a plan, purely under the feeling of a commission, and in this way chapter after chapter has come into being. The work involved has helped me to endure in faith this war, for me the most grievous of the three.[17]

An analysis of the beginnings of Christianity to understand its essential nature as a way of a commencement of a dialogue from the Jewish side was also the method used by Joseph Klausner.[18]

David Flusser was one of those who through research of the sources tried to understand the past in order to shape a future relation. He concludes and affirms that "only from the Synoptic Gospels do we know the faith *of* Jesus; outside them, it is the faith *in* Christ that is mostly presented and developed."[19] He says,

> Paul was the most important factor in a trend which gave birth to Christianity as a distinct religion, because he deepened its Christology and stressed the inevitable necessity of accepting it for salvation, and he was the most extreme exponent of the doctrine that the Jewish way of life had no validity for Christians. The Gentile Christians in Rome, to whom Paul wrote his epistle, were

---

16. Buber, *Two Types*, 173–74.
17. Ibid., 15.
18. Klausner, *MiYeshu 'ad Paulus*.
19. Flusser, *Judaism and the Origins of Christianity*, 622.

surely Gentile God-fearers before becoming Christians: e.g., they knew the Old Testament (Rom 7:1). Paul's opinion is that, by being converted to Christianity, they "have died to the law by becoming identified with the body of Christ."[20]

Finally, he remarks,

> On the other hand, the origin of Christianity is Jewish, and many of the first Gentile Christians were close to Judaism; Jesus and his disciples were observant Jews: therefore Christianity had to solve the problem of why the Jewish people did not embrace Christianity. The separation of Christianity from Judaism was brought about by heightening the centrifugal tendency, which produced opposition to and even hatred of Jews in Gentile Christians. The Jewish origin of Christianity and the failure of Christianity to convert the Jewish people to the new message was precisely the reason for the strong anti-Jewish trend in Christianity; this explains the disharmony between the old and new community, which is probably unique in the history of religions . . . Tension towards Judaism was an historical necessity for Christianity, in order to become a world religion for former pagans—a need which no longer exists. Today, Christianity can renew itself out of Judaism and with the help of Judaism. Then it will become a humane religion.[21]

The challenge left for us by all those who have looked into the sources of Christianity is to continue looking in them for new perspectives.

There is a story in the Talmud in which it is possible to distinguish the two components of Christianity described by Buber and Flusser. In *Shabbat* 116a, b we read as follows:

> Imma Shalom, R. Eliezer's wife, was R. Gamaliel's sister. Now, a certain philosopher lived in his vicinity and he bore a reputation that he did not accept bribes. They wished to expose him, so she brought him a golden lamp, went before him, [and] said to him, "I desire that a share be given me in my [deceased] father's estate." "Divide," ordered he. Said he [R. Gamaliel] to him, "It is decreed for us, 'Where there is a son, a daughter does not inherit.'" [He replied], "Since the day that you were exiled from your land the Law of Moses has been superseded and *another book given*, wherein it is written, 'A son and a daughter inherit equally.'" The next day, he [R. Gamaliel] brought him a Lybian ass. Said he to them, "Look at

20. Ibid., 631.
21. Ibid., 644.

the end of the book, wherein it is written, 'I came not to destroy the Law of Moses nor to add to the law of Moses,' and it is written therein, 'A daughter does not inherit where there is a son.'" Said R. Gamaliel to him, "An ass came and knocked the lamp over!"[22]

Undoubtedly, the story is referring to an encounter involving R. Gamaliel and his wife, Imma Shalom, well known in the Talmudic sources for her cleverness,[23] with a member of the Christian congregation at the end of the first century or beginning of the second, if we consider the story to be real and not a legend based on a reality of later times. The word translated here as "philosopher" appears as *philosopha* (פילוסופא) in this Talmudic text. In some other rabbinical texts, the word *philosophos* (פילוסופוס) appears as referring to thinkers whose concepts could identify them as belonging to the first Christian congregations,[24] and in others, with pagan ideas.[25]

The words "another book given" appear in the Oxford Codex as "and the law of the Evangelium has been given." There is no passage in any known Gospel in which a son and daughter inherit alike, and the Gospel passage alluded to seems to be Matthew 5:17ff.

The story could be understood as a harsh criticism against those who put aside the Law, arguing that Judea's destruction by the Romans ended the validity of the Law of the Torah. But it presents in an uncritical way the teachings of Jesus, who affirmed that Moses's Torah must be kept. The views of the Jewish Christians and the Gentile Christians seem to be presented in this story.

Another very analyzed story of the Talmud, which shows the similar image of Jews and Christians that Romans had, appears in *Avodah Zarah* 16b–17a. Rabbi Elie'zer ben Hurkanos, we are told in this *agadah*, was arrested by the Romans on the charge of being a Christian. After his liberation, he realized that he had been punished by God for the sin of feeling pleasure from the words of a disciple of Jesus from Nazareth.[26]

---

22. Epstein, Babylonian Talmud, *Shabbat* 116a, b.

23. Epstein, Babylonian Talmud, *Nedarim* 20a; *Bava Metzi'a* 59, 2; Masekhtot Ketanot, Kalah 1:10 (Kalah Rabati 1:15).

24. Kalah Rabati 7:4; Sifre Devarim, Parashat Haazinu 307 D"H: Davar Aḥer; Bereshit Raba, Parashat Bereshit, Parashah 11, Siman 6. In Goldwurm and Scherman, *Talmud Bavli*.

25. Bereshit Raba, Parashat Bereshit, Parashah 1, D"H: Bereshit bara. In Theodor and Albeck, *Midrash Bereshit rabah*.

26. Boyarin, *Dying for God*, 26–49.

The ambivalence described in this *agadah* characterizes the deep concern Jews have had about Christians during the last twenty centuries.

An astonishing example of this ambivalence in the interpretation of certain passages of the rabbinic sources can be seen in the understanding of Ben Petora's point of view in his discussion with Rabbi Akiva, as it appears in *Bava Metzi'a* 62a:

> Now how does R. Johanan interpret, "*that thy brother may live with thee.*"[27] He utilizes it for that which was taught: If two are travelling on a journey [far from civilization], and one has a pitcher of water—if both drink, they will [both] die, but if one only drinks, he can reach civilization—the son of Patura taught: It is better that both should drink and die, rather than that one should behold his companion's death. Until R. Akiba came and taught: "*that thy brother may live* with *thee*": thy life takes precedence over his life.[28]

Ahad Ha'Am[29] identifies Ben Petora's opinion as a Christian one; Malbim (Meir Leibush ben Iehiel Mikhl Wissel, 1809–79)[30] understood that Ben A'zai has the same opinion as Ben Petora. This dual interpretation is understandable, especially if we understand that the first Christian congregations were in close dialogue with the rabbinical milieu of that time and that they shared with rabbis many points of view. This is seen, among many others, in the parallels pointed out by Gedaliahu Alon,[31] between rabbinical sources from the first century and the *Didache*.

The future of Christian-Jewish dialogue lies in resuming, and renewing, the old dialogue, which was disrupted almost two thousand years ago. Of course, it is impossible to restart the dialogue at the same point at which it was broken off and disregard all that happened during the succeeding two thousand years. But the challenge for each side is to see the other as a partner in the struggle of a common challenge: to install a dimension of spirituality in the midst of humanity, erasing idolatry in all its forms from human reality.

In the words of Rabbi Abraham Joshua Heschel,

---

27. Lev 25:36.
28. Flusser, *Judaism and the Origins of Christianity*, 631.
29. Ha'Am, "Al shtei ha-se'ipim," 46.
30. HaTorah VehaMitzvah, at the end of his commentary to Sifra in the verse "Veahavta LeRea'kha Kamokha."
31. Alon, "Teaching of the Twelve Apostles," 274–94.

> Nazism has suffered a defeat, but the process of eliminating the Bible from the consciousness of the Western world goes on. It is on the issue of saving the radiance of the Hebrew Bible in the minds of man that Jews and Christians are called upon to work together. *None of us can do it alone.*[32]

For Catholics, the new approach and dialogue with Jews based on the *Nostra aetate* theological statements open a theological quest. What does the "Old Testament" mean for them now, taking into account that the old covenant with the Jewish people is still valid?

For Jews, this means to take closer to heart Maimonides' statement in his authoritative Code:

> It is beyond the human mind to fathom the designs of the Creator; for our ways are not His ways, neither are our thoughts His thoughts. All these matters relating to Jesus of Nazareth and the Ishmaelite (Mohammed) who came after him served to clear the way for King Messiah, to prepare the whole world to worship God with one accord, as it is written, "For then will I turn to the peoples a pure language, that they may all call upon the name of the Lord to serve Him with one consent" (Zephaniah 3:9). Thus the messianic hope, the Torah, and the commandments have become familiar topics—topics of conversation (among the inhabitants) of the far isles and many peoples . . .[33]

There is still a long way before us until *Nostra aetate* in its body and spirit will be incorporated into the heart of all the churches and parishes throughout the world. But still, the next step must be to think and to analyze the present dramatic moment in humankind's history in order to continue paving a way for a better future.

---

32. Heschel, "No Religion Is an Island," 236.
33. Hilkhot Melakhim 11:4, cited in Heschel, "No Religion Is an Island," 248–49.

4

Understanding Pope Francis

Roots and Horizons of Church Reform

ALLAN FIGUEROA DECK, SJ

Few can deny that the first year of Pope Francis's papacy has been nothing less than spectacular. Has the Church or, for that matter, the world experienced anything quite like it in recent memory? The Church and the world have been watching as the first Latin American and Jesuit pope reveals his vision for them, one that is not altogether predictable, leaves space for both change and orthodoxy—creative fidelity—and enjoys an unprecedented amount of success in terms of the communication and reception of his message. This presentation is a modest attempt to explore the background of an extraordinary man and his way of proceeding by identifying the sources of and emerging directions for the reform he leads.

The first section profiles his birth to Italian immigrant parents in Argentina. The second considers the impact of Jesuit formation, especially his exposure to the distinctive spirituality of St. Ignatius of Loyola. A third section highlights the ecclesial context that marked the most decisive periods in Bergoglio's life; and the fourth specifically refers to the theology of the people, an Argentine version of liberation theology that flourished in the pope's formative years and now gains recognition as a key to the pope's theological vision. A fifth section calls attention to key experiences during his tenure as archbishop of Buenos Aires, and a sixth points out the enduring impact on the future pope of his experience at the Fifth Conference of the Bishops of Latin America and the Caribbean at Aparecida, Brazil, in 2007. This, of course, is part of a bigger piece that is the extraordinarily rich experience of the Church in Latin America in the years after the Second Vatican Council. The seventh and final section highlights some major changes in pastoral care, tone and style that the pope's vision of reform implies.[1]

Argentine, Immigrant Roots

Jorge Mario Bergoglio's family roots are immigrant and lower middle class. This helps one understand the profound sympathy he has for people on the margins. Like any immigrant group, the Bergoglios experienced the sense of dislocation and anomie that is so characteristic of the immigrant story. Moreover, in the years immediately prior to Jorge Mario's birth, the family experienced the effects of the worldwide economic depression of the 1930s. This period coincided with the rise of the charismatic Juan Domingo Perón and, perhaps even more pertinent, with the extraordinary phenomenon of his wife Evita, who was idolized by the entire Argentine society, but most especially by the poor. Moreover, among his parish priests the young Jorge Mario came to know Salesians who undoubtedly communicated something of their founder Don Bosco's passion for the service to the poor, for youth, and for Catholic social doctrine as inspired by Pope Leo XIII. The social ethos of Bergoglio's early years and youth was charged with concern for workers, students, and with the passionate political activism of Peronism at its birth.[2]

Consequently in the 1940s, the formative years of Jorge Mario's youth, the foundation for the extraordinary grip, the fascination and resilience that Peronism has enjoyed in Argentina was set in place. Peronism shaped a great deal of Bergoglio's political consciousness. At least two distinctive features of it have marked the *modus operandi* of Bergoglio: first, the central role given to the popular masses—the *pueblo*—in Bergoglio's thought and

---

1. A veritable cottage industry of publications has developed around the new pope. Spanish-language writers have had an inside track on the sources since virtually all of the main ones are in Spanish. Given the close relationship of Pope Francis to theologian and now Archbishop Victor Manuel Fernández, rector of the Catholic University of Argentina, Paolo Rodari's interview with the archbishop is particularly authoritative. See Fernández and Rodari, *El programa del Papa Francisco*.

2. For a description of the complexity of the relations of the Church with Peronism in the first decade, see Bergoglio and Skorka, *On Heaven and Earth*, 205–9.

action; and second, his unwavering concern for the poor, for matters of social justice and for human dignity. In Perón's case one might ask to what extent Perón's rhetoric was just another example of the scourge of populism that in Latin America often becomes more a tool for the manipulation of the masses than a sincere commitment to them followed with coherent action. Some of Bergoglio's opponents within the Argentine Church and beyond have expressed concern for what they see as this kind of populism in Bergoglio's rhetoric and style.³

Pope Francis is not just an Argentine patriot but more importantly he is a *porteño*, that is, a resident of Buenos Aires practically all his life with the exception of a few years in which the Jesuits sent him to study in Chile and Germany and briefly carry out pastoral ministry in Córdoba. Perhaps no other pope in history is the product of an immense, cosmopolitan urban environment like that of greater Buenos Aires, one of the ten most densely populated urban centers of the world, and certainly among the top—if not the top—cultural and artistic centers of Latin America.⁴ Argentina has a long history of immigration and is, along with Brazil, the most culturally diverse nation in Latin America. While firmly Catholic in tradition, Argentina is also ecumenical and interreligious—this is true of Buenos Aires, in particular—with thriving churches of various Christian denominations, Islamic mosques, and Jewish synagogues. It is also a significantly secular city, even though Catholic history and symbolic expressions are omnipresent. Interestingly enough, in the Americas, Buenos Aires is rivaled only by New York in terms of Jewish population. Cardinal Bergoglio was known for his frequent meeting with people of all faiths, for his presence in their places of worship, and for his many dealings and friendships with people of other religions. Most notable is the deep, brotherly affection between Pope Francis and the leading rabbi of Buenos Aires, Abraham Skorka.

Bergoglio the Jesuit

At the age of twenty-one, Bergoglio entered the Jesuit order after a brief period of study in the diocesan seminary that was staffed by Jesuits. Around

---

3. Despite the sensationalist subtitles, of the several good biographies of Bergoglio, perhaps the most incisive and evocative are Vallely, *Pope Francis*, and Larraquy, *Recen por él*.

4. The urban pastoral concerns of Bergoglio are ascribed to his deep *porteño* roots by Galli, "Ternura, alegría, conversion y reforma."

this time he suffered a severe lung problem that brought him near death. Soon after his convalescence he entered the Jesuit novitiate. He was a bright, zealous, and energetic young man who most people would say "was going places." All his life he stood out as leader, and when large numbers of both older and younger Jesuits left the Order in the turbulent years of the late sixties and seventies after the Second Vatican Council, Jorge Mario came to the attention of his superiors, including Father General Pedro Arrupe in Rome. At this point began his spectacular ascendancy to novice director, provincial, superior of the Colegio Máximo, and on to auxiliary bishop and soon archbishop of Buenos Aires and primate of Argentina.

While unquestionably a man of great generosity and ambition, the future pope demonstrated great interest and love for Ignatian spirituality. As novice director for three years, provincial superior, and then again superior of the large community of Jesuits at San Miguel, a Buenos Aires suburb, his approach to ministry was markedly practical as distinct from theological or speculative. For him, spirituality integrates theory with practice, ideas with reality, prayer with action. He is a man of action more than ideas, blending spirituality with pastoral sensitivity in an almost seamless manner. This shows itself in a tendency to place a premium on reality and human experience. He avoids ideology as much as possible. This is what helps explain the fact that he has had critics from both extremes of the political spectrum: from the left during the dangerous Cold War years of military dictatorships in Latin America, and from the right in his fifteen-year tenure as archbishop when he went *mano a mano* with the Roman dicasteries, with some prominent Argentine prelates, and not infrequently with the governments of Néstor Kirchner and his wife, Cristina Fernández.[5] The ecclesiastics found his love of the poor and antipathy for clericalism and the regal trappings of church office more than a little disturbing. They interpreted all this as an aberration and ascribed it to his Peronist tendencies. When entrusted with the leadership of the entire Argentine Province of the Jesuits during the dangerous years of military dictatorship, he did not position the Jesuits in the opposing camp, nor did he publically protest the cruel violence and injustices of the generals. Like Pope Pius XII during World War II, Bergoglio stayed as best he could in the good graces of the generals while

---

5. A rather remarkable discussion of Bergoglio's struggle with Roman dicasteries and certain Argentine ecclesiastics throughout his tenure as archbishop is found in Piqué, *Francisco*, 141–60. Even more revealing is the candid discussion of Bergoglio's Argentine ecclesiastical adversaries in Fernández, "Bergoglio a secas." See also Vallely, *Pope Francis*, 1–21.

doing all he could to help those they were so cruelly oppressing. One might argue that in this he demonstrated a sense of "discrete charity," a term used in Ignatian spirituality to refer to discernment that requires much prayer, study, and prudence.

The root of Bergoglio's pastoral and spiritual concerns may best be ascribed to basic principles of Ignatian spirituality, which seek to integrate a person's deepest concerns into a coherent and authentic pattern of life. Indeed, Bergoglio is relentless in his disdain for anything that smacks of Phariseeism. He sees too much of this in the Church itself. Fundamentally the superficiality of Phariseeism manifests the shadow side of religion, one that provides a person and even the entire ecclesial institution with customs and rituals that sometimes substitute for a deeper integration of faith with life and obscure rather than give witness to an authentic relationship of love for God and others. Nothing can substitute for a life of reflection and prayer in community, one that is open to conversion over a lifetime. For five centuries, people—not all of them Catholic or even Christian—have found this call to authenticity in the Spiritual Exercises of St. Ignatius very attractive. The appeal and power of Pope Francis has everything to do with the spiritual integration that this man exudes.

Similarly, Pope Francis's orientation toward openness and willingness to change is grounded in the notion of discernment which is central to Ignatian spirituality. This refers to the ongoing effort to respond lovingly and generously to God's will in one's life by monitoring one's decisions—what one does with her time, money, and talents. Discernment requires a proper regard for reality and intelligence—inquiry about the facts, openness to change, consultation with others, and readiness to reflect and pray. More than anything else, Ignatian discernment demands a profound degree of *liberty* in the individual. One way to gain this kind of *freedom for* rather than *freedom from* is found in the cultivation of what St. Ignatius calls *indifference*. This requires an ability to identify one's deepest motivations and desires and determine whether they are leading one toward God or away from God. Ignatius proposes the idea that our lives and actions, if we are truly following Christ, must derive from our deepest and most authentic desires, that is, from the good spirit of light rather than from the bad spirit of darkness. The most characteristic Ignatian method of prayer is the Examen of Consciousness, which Jesuits and other practitioners use on a daily basis precisely for the purpose of identifying and purifying their motives and cultivating generosity toward God and others.

Pope Francis's leadership style is marked by a strong orientation toward discernment. He continually proposes for his own use and for that of all leaders in the Church a method that requires a radical kind of openness to God's will. Perhaps this radical freedom at the heart of the Jesuit and Ignatian heritage explains an aura of revolution or radical change that has haunted Jesuits throughout history—not just in the Vatican II era—and given them a disturbing edge and made them controversial on countless occasions over the centuries. One might argue that this Jesuit indifference is exactly what was needed to get the Church back on the track of dialogue with the world and serious reform of structures. Pope Francis intends to move the Church forward to where Christ is beckoning.[6] The resignation of Pope Benedict obviously signaled that something was terribly wrong at the Vatican, and the cardinals at the conclave realized that Jorge Mario Bergoglio—with God's help—had both the integrity and the steeliness to correct it.

The Ecclesial Context

Theologian Massimo Faggioli has observed that the acceptance given to the reforms of the Second Vatican Council by the Latin American bishops gathered in Medellín for their Second General Conference in 1968 was "the largest effort of a continental church for a creative reception of the Council."[7] This openness to Vatican II on the part of the Latin American bishops was due to several factors. One of the first was a growing recognition that the Catholicism of Latin America was running out of steam in the face of technological, economic, and political change. The paradigm of Christendom fostered by the *patronato real* and the colonial experience of the Church in Latin America was problematical in the face of rising modernity. Hence the Second Vatican Council's call for dialogue with the world in *Gaudium et spes* was urgently necessary for engaging the changing circumstances of Latin America in a hopeful, constructive manner. Similarly, the vision of the Church as People of God in history as asserted by *Lumen gentium* resonated with the idiosyncrasy of Latin America's strong, distinctive religious ethos called popular Catholicism. *Gaudium et spes*, the Pastoral Constitution on the Church in the Modern World,

6. Martin, "His Way of Proceeding," 16–18. For many leads on how to connect Pope Francis's way of proceeding and his Jesuit spirituality, see also Lowney, *Pope Francis*.

7. Faggioli, *Vatican II*, 54.

gave a role of central importance to culture in the anthropological sense of the word. It made culture the target of the Church's mission and identity, which is to evangelize. Much more was to be said about this later in Paul VI's Apostolic Exhortation *Evangelii nuntiandi*. The prevalence of many rituals, symbols, and narratives in Latin American Catholicism—many of them products of a remarkable process of inculturation or hybridization—made this form of Catholicism an especially rich treasure chest of reflection and outreach to the popular masses. The Vatican Council's strong commitment to Catholic social doctrine, to socioeconomic justice for all as demonstrated in major documents like Pope Paul VI's *Populorum progressio* and the Synod on Justice in 1971, resonated well with the growing realization of Latin America's economic dependency, grinding poverty, and lack of democracy. All of these factors came together to create a climate of serious dialogue among the bishops themselves, the clergy, and a growing number of laity. Bergoglio's years of study for the priesthood and his first years as priest coincided with this heady time of Vatican II reforms, which decidedly stamped his vision of the Church. The fact that the Jesuit Colegio Máximo at San Miguel became the center of much of this dialogue helps explain the profoundly dialogical and open stance he regularly took with regard to matters of church life. His vision is simply not one of looking back. He calls himself a "son of the Church," which refers to his commitment to the authentic teachings of Catholicism.[8] But he is quick to recall Saint John XXIII's observation in his inaugural discourse at the Second Vatican Council that "the substance of the deposit of faith is one thing, but the way in which it is presented is another."[9]

While there were traditionalist movements in the Church in Argentina and elsewhere throughout Latin America during the period after the Second Vatican Council, the simple fact is that they gained limited traction there for a host of reasons related to the realization that the old models of Christendom that underpin these movements were not particularly relevant to the changed realities of life, to the rising prospects of the poor and marginal populations of the continent, nor to the teeming masses and the attraction to modernity of Latin America's youth and young adults. Pope Francis's lack of enthusiasm for the Latin Mass other than as a beautiful relic or "museum piece" is the result of giving more importance to the pastoral challenges of reality than to restorationist ideologies.

8. See Spadaro, "A Big Heart Open to God."
9. See Pope John XXIII, "Opening Speech."

Perhaps as pertinent to the Latin American Church's focus on engagement with the world in the years immediately following Vatican II was the profound influence of the Young Christian Workers that brought the influential vision of Cardinal Joseph Cardijn's "see-judge-act" methodology to Latin America in the decades preceding the Council. This vision emphasized dialogue with history and social sciences in the engagement with local and national realities and in the discovery of pastoral remedies to the challenges facing the wider Church. These movements galvanized an entire generation of Catholic leaders—clergy and laity—through associations like the Young Christian Workers, Young Christian Students, and Catholic Action. An extraordinary flowering of Catholic lay leaders throughout Latin America, including Argentina, took place in the first part of the twentieth century—Bergoglio's formative years. The Young Catholic Workers and Catholic Action were effective instruments for the dissemination of Catholic social doctrine as first promulgated by Pope Leo XIII. These movements engaged the socioeconomic and political contexts of many Latin American nations as they evolved in the middle of the twentieth century. While Argentina was a deeply traditional Catholic country and the Church enjoyed status among many of the ruling elites of the nation, Bergoglio's formative years were a time of rapid change and new ideas that focused on the popular masses more than on the elites.

The iconic figure of Cardinal Eduardo Pironio best represents this new current of forward leadership that arose in Latin America in the exciting years immediately after the Second Vatican Council when Bergoglio was completing his theological studies and preparing for ordination. Pironio was the most famous Argentine churchman of the times, a revered seminary professor and rector who later became bishop of Mar del Plata, General Secretary and then President of CELAM, the Conference of Latin American Bishops. Pironio was an extraordinary example of a dedicated, forward-looking prelate who was highly favored by Pope Paul VI and made president of the Congregation of the Laity by Saint John Paul II. Pironio promoted the vision of CELAM's historic conferences at Medellín and Puebla, which squarely committed the Church in Latin America to a preferential option for the poor.[10]

---

10. See Eduardo Pironio's influential writings in the early 1970s, which disseminated the message of Medellín throughout Latin America. For example, Pironio, *La iglesia en América Latina*; also Galli, "Introducción," 3–11.

Argentine Liberation Theology and Theology of the People

What was the role of theology in general and liberation theology in particular in the formation of Jorge Mario Bergoglio's understanding of his faith? To answer this question, it is necessary to go back to those years in San Miguel in and around the time of the Second Vatican Council. This was a period of ferment in which very capable thinkers like Juan Carlos Scannone, Lucio Gera, and Rafael Tello emerged as significant leaders of the theological academy in dialogue with the life of the Church. Undoubtedly, Jorge Mario breathed in some of the passion and originality of these prolific teachers and writers. However, it is true that Bergoglio opposed a certain brand of liberation theology. He was opposed to it insofar as many of its proponents were highly ideological and identified by many in the highly fraught period of political and military violence of the 1970s and 1980s as a source of communist-inspired revolution. This was the period of the national security state that arose in the *Cono Sur*—Chile, Brazil, Argentina, Paraguay, and Uruguay—and in Central America. These nations came under the grip of nasty military regimes abetted, no doubt, by US hemispheric Cold War concerns about international communism. As a young Jesuit thrust too early into his order's leadership as provincial superior, Bergoglio "made mistakes and was authoritarian," as he himself confesses.[11] Nevertheless, many would agree that Bergoglio did what was prudentially necessary given the utter ruthlessness of the military regime. The fact is that Bergoglio changed his mind about liberation theology when the political context changed and when he came to see its coherence with clearly established values that he regarded very highly in the theology of the people espoused by revered professors like Gera, Tello, and Scannone. As has been pointed out, the theology of the people might properly be considered an Argentine form of liberation theology, the main difference between the two theologies being the former's rejection of the latter's Marxist analytical tools and emphasis on socioeconomic issues rather than on the anthropological concept of culture and the notion of "the people" as championed by Gera and others.[12]

In connection with Bergoglio's attitude toward liberation theology, it is important to note that he has always been deeply interested in politics

---

11. Spadaro, "A Big Heart Open to God."
12. Scannone, "Perspectivas eclesiológicas."

understood as the art of the possible—making things happen. As a youth he was exposed to the thought and rhetoric of international communism, as he mentioned in his *America* interview—something quite normal in the life of an informed, engaged Argentinian of his times. As already mentioned, the most prominent churchman of Bergoglio's early years of formation as a Jesuit was Eduardo Pironio, later to become cardinal and promoter of the conclusions of both the Medellín and Puebla conferences. Years later, Bergoglio was to become a key player at a similar conference of all the bishops at Aparecida, at which the preferential option for the poor was reiterated in the strongest possible terms.[13] Bergoglio is inexplicable without reference to CELAM's heritage, within which he is most firmly grounded.

The Faculty of Theology at the Catholic University of Argentina (UCA) in Buenos Aires is the home of several outstanding theologians. Among them was Lucio Gera, who is considered the father of *teología del pueblo*, which is also called Argentine liberation theology. Gera passed away in 2012. Cardinal Bergoglio thought so highly of Gera that on his death he arranged for his burial in the crypt of the bishops of Buenos Aires. This created quite a stir in the area because Gera was closely identified with Argentine liberation theology and the option for the poor. In his fifteen years of service as archbishop of Buenos Aires, Bergoglio served as chancellor of the Catholic University and had many contacts with its distinguished faculty. Among them was a diocesan priest from the region of Córdoba by the name of Victor Manuel Fernández, who worked closely with Bergoglio in the writing of the document of Aparecida. Bergoglio was president of the editorial committee that produced the final document. Carlos María Galli, another diocesan priest of Buenos Aires and former dean of the UCA Faculty of Theology, also collaborated with the committee in this task. Virginia Azcuy, also of the UCA theology faculty, is part of this community of scholars who study Gera and Tello and remain connected with Pope Francis and involved in some of the more significant scholarly analysis of the pope's writings. Victor Fernández was appointed rector of the Catholic University by Cardinal Bergoglio, and a few weeks after his election the new pope named him titular archbishop

---

13. A fascinating discussion of the theological currents that influenced Bergoglio is found in Bianchi, *Pobres en este mundo*, a penetrating study of the seminal theology of Rafael Tello, one of the more influential theologians of the second half of the twentieth century in Argentina. Cardinal Bergoglio wrote the prologue to this book in which he extols the thought of Tello, one of the leading thinkers of the *teología del pueblo*, or Argentine liberation theology as it is sometimes called.

while remaining rector of the Catholic University. He is known to collaborate with Pope Francis in the pope's communications. Anyone desirous of greater insight regarding the sources and tendencies of Bergoglio's theological vision need go no further than the UCA, where a core group of the theologians who have influenced him are to be found.

To the primary role of Lucio Gera in the forging of Bergoglio's thought must be added the name of Rafael Tello. This theologian's situation is quite curious. He had problems not only with the military dictators who silenced him but also with Cardinal Aramburu, his archbishop and, at the time, archbishop of Buenos Aires. Tello had a significant impact on Gera's teachings regarding *teología del pueblo*, but Tello published very little. For many years he did not openly practice the priesthood and lived ostracized in his own house. For decades, nevertheless, students came to speak with him, and he gave workshops that were often audio-recorded; and recently transcriptions of his lectures have been published.[14] What connects Tello with the other Argentine theologians already mentioned is a strong pastoral/theological focus, an expressed desire to integrate theory and praxis—something much less common for European or US theologians. Many of these Argentine theologians were diocesan priests who practically always exercised direct parish and other ministerial functions; their teaching and writing reflects a remarkable concern for doing serious, substantive theological reflection solidly based on reality and experience as well as on the best scriptural and doctrinal sources. These frequently classify themselves as systematic *and* pastoral theologians, a combination that is fairly rare in the mainstream European and US theological world.

A lifelong associate of Pope Francis is the leading Jesuit Argentine philosopher Juan Carlos Scannone, who maintains that the *teología del pueblo* has made a great impact on the pope. This theology stresses the People of God as evangelists, as the basic protagonists of the Church's mission, which begins with the proclamation of the kerygma and the joyous Christ of Easter. Many elements of this theology are found in the Church's teaching on evangelization and the new evangelization in the two preceding papacies, but in an obvious way in the magna carta of Pope Francis's *Evangelii gaudium*.

---

14. Tello, *Pueblo y cultura popular*.

Archbishop of Buenos Aires

Bergoglio served as auxiliary bishop of Buenos Aires from 1992 to 1997 and as archbishop from that year to 2013—twenty-one years in total. He was the first Jesuit ever to serve in this capacity. He came to be deeply loved by the ordinary people because he consistently showed a special concern for the people on the margin with unequivocal actions like missioning some of his best priests to the *villas de miseria*, as the slums of greater Buenos Aires are called. Along with this, he exhibited a personal interest in the poorest of the poor by visiting them wherever they were to be found and even celebrating Mass in a plaza or close to a trash dump where many poor people were to be found. In addition, as is well known, he preferred to use public transportation—the bus or the metro—wherever he went. The archbishop's car remained in the garage, and his residence was a small apartment shared with a couple of other priests. Bergoglio often cooked for himself. Even though he was Argentina's leading prelate, he generally shunned travel, especially international travel, and "kept his nose to the grindstone."

As archbishop, Bergoglio revealed a love for the clergy and concern for their well-being, along with a persistent antipathy for any form of clericalism. This did not earn him the admiration of some clerics, especially in Argentina where certain sectors of the clergy were used to privileges deriving from their social class origins, family connections, and dealings with the Catholic aristocracy. In Argentina and elsewhere, bishops and priests may sometimes cultivate wealthy patrons and practice clientelism. Bergoglio's preference for service to the poor and underserved was clearly a threat to this practice. Understandably, the more affluent sectors of *porteño* society may have felt abandoned by their archbishop, who showed esteem for them, too, but paid more attention to the downtrodden. Many priests of the archdiocese were quite devoted to Bergoglio, but he did shake them up more than once with his frequent calls for a truly missionary church always in outreach, *siempre en salida*.

Pope Francis likes to tell the story about a sociologist who reported that the typical parish has influence in an area about six hundred meters in radius. In Buenos Aires, the parishes are on the average two thousand meters distant from each other. In light of this Cardinal Bergoglio casually proposed in conversation that some pastors think about forming laity to provide catechetical and perhaps eucharistic ministries for the sick and other services outside the parish—for example, in storefronts or garages in the neighborhoods. Many pastors did not like this idea and complained that if they did that the people would not come to Mass. To this the archbishop replied, "What do you mean? Suddenly all these people are going to Mass?" For Bergoglio the urgency of a missionary option that fosters a "culture of encounter" within the Church at all levels, an *iglesia en salida*, was already a guiding principle for his years of pastoral ministry as bishop.[15]

Another prominent feature of his ministry was his persistent promotion of ecumenism and interreligious dialogue. Together with Catholic charismatics, whom he came to regard very highly (unlike some of his brother bishops and priests), Bergoglio visited ecumenical gatherings and cultivated deeper relationships with many distinct denominations. A case in point is the Anglican Pentecostal Bishop Tony Palmer, whom Pope Francis has known for years. The pope appeared live via video conference from Rome with Bishop Palmer and hundreds of Pentecostal ministers meeting in Dallas, Texas. In Buenos Aires, Archbishop Bergoglio was known to visit Pentecostal and other Protestant churches and to receive them for ecumenical services in the cathedral. Incidentally, the picture of Bergoglio kneeling down to receive a blessing from Argentine Pentecostal ministers caused a stir among traditionalists who maintain that by doing so the archbishop *ipso facto* incurred excommunication! Relations with Islamic leaders were also quite cordial, not to speak of relations with the Jewish community, which were excellent. Much more surely can and should be said about Pope Francis's remarkable record of pastoral ministry in his hectic but infinitely creative and productive years as chief pastor in Buenos Aires.

Aparecida

In some ways, the 2007 gathering of the bishops of Latin America and the Caribbean in Aparecida, Brazil, was a watershed moment in the life and ministry of Jorge Mario Bergoglio. He thoroughly immersed himself in the process and became the single most influential exponent of the Aparecida Conference's conclusions, which on his ascendency to the papacy have come to play an essential role in the articulation of the content and methodology of his project, his radical vision of a thoroughly missionary Church. As chairman of the commission entrusted with writing the final Aparecida document, Bergoglio and his team plunged into the task of composing a two-hundred-page book that recapitulates and goes well beyond the vision

15. See the in-depth interviews of Cardinal Bergoglio regarding his way of life as chief shepherd of Buenos Aires in Rubin and Ambrogetti, *El jesuita*.

forged by the profoundly influential documents of CELAM's Medellín and Puebla. To accomplish this, he worked feverishly with a team of theologians (mentioned above) in whom he has great confidence. Much can and should be said about the Aparecida Conference. For the purposes of brevity only a few factors will be highlighted. The first is that the controversy regarding the see-judge-act methodology so identified with the pastoral orientation of the Church in Latin America and liberation theology was vigorously reaffirmed. This happened despite the efforts of some cautious ecclesial elements—abetted perhaps by forces in Rome who were always somewhat ill at ease with the vision of Medellín and Puebla and with the legacy of liberation theology—to pretend it had died or gone out of style. Pope Benedict XVI, however, on his arrival at Aparecida, confirmed two signature aspects of CELAM's historic pastoral vision: the see-judge-act, inductive pastoral methodology and the option for the poor, which Benedict actually reinforced with a strong christological approach to the theme at the assembly's opening discourse.

In addition to the endorsement of CELAM's inductive pastoral methodology, Aparecida proposed several key notions that Pope Francis has made foundational for his vision of change for the entire Church, not just the Church in Latin America. Only four key themes or ideas of Aparecida to be found in Pope Francis's many references to it will be noted here. The first is the *missionary identity* of the Church. The Church exists for the purpose of reaching out, going out—*iglesia en salida*. This point was already made by Pope Paul VI in *Evangelii nuntiandi*; St. John Paul II underscored the idea in *Redemptoris missio*, but Aparecida took it more to heart and thought through its implications arguably more than any other ecclesial document until *Evangelii gaudium*. In this apostolic exhortation, Pope Francis enshrines these and several other key concepts of Aparecida. Indeed, there are twenty references to Aparecida in *Evangelii gaudium*.[16]

A second important notion from Aparecida is *pastoral conversion*, which refers to the need for reforms at many levels in the Church. The reform must be inspired on the inductive methodology of CELAM, which seeks to integrate the primarily religious purpose of the Church with its human underpinnings, to transcend the dualisms of faith and science, the social and the spiritual, spirit and matter, and the human and the divine that render so much preaching and teaching in the Church ineffective. The two central mysteries of the Incarnation and the Resurrection, especially

---

16. See Galli, "Papa Francisco," 14.

the joy of the Risen Christ, are given pride of place in Pope Francis's program of *pastoral conversion*. Involved in this as well is the achievement of a better tone and balance in the *communication* of Church teaching—for instance, by projecting the kerygma, God's mercy, and the joy of the Risen Christ first rather than moralisms about matters of sexual morality.

A third key concept is *missionary disciples*. This idea alludes to the inadequacy of the distinction between clergy and laity. Following the lead of Vatican II's *Lumen gentium*, Aparecida insists on *missionary disciples* being the most useful general term to refer to all the faithful, who by virtue of baptism are called to missionary discipleship with the Lord. The failure to clarify this fundamental reality of baptismal identity as a result of a great deal of clericalism in the Church is seriously challenged by Aparecida. Now Pope Francis is doing just that for the entire Church. Indeed, a disquieting realization raised by this term *missionary disciples* being applied to all the baptized is that widespread clerical structures have had the undesirable effect of depriving the Church of its radical missionary identity by relegating outreach and leadership to a relatively small group of persons, the clergy and a handful of subordinated workers. The Church's mission simply cannot be carried out effectively under these conditions. Of concern here as well is the fact that in some ways the role of women in this mission has not yet been adequately developed. On several occasions, Pope Francis has mentioned the need to think more deeply about the role of women in the Church because the failure to do so hinders the Church's becoming "entirely missionary."

A fourth influential theme used in Aparecida that is now having an impact on the universal Church are the New Testament stories about Samaritans. In Spanish, the word *samaritanidad*—"Samaritanness"—has been coined.[17] This is a very rich reference that serves as an umbrella for many key concepts that inspire Pope Francis. One of these concepts is the need to promote a *culture of encounter* in the Church and the world rather than a *culture of war* mentality. The Good Samaritan is the person who does not even profess the faith of Israel—and, indeed, is much despised—and yet does the right thing. The Samaritan manifests in deeds the requirement of love. The Samaritan Woman at the Well is the one who enjoys a remarkable dialogue with the other who is Christ, and vice versa, thus giving the

---

17. Cardinal Oscar Rodríguez Maradiaga refers to the culture of the Good Samaritan in his description of the new evangelization in the spirit of Pope Francis's reform in Rodríguez Maradiaga, "Importance of the New Evangelization," 5.3.

example of openness to dialogue that is respectful and transcends the limits of cultural, gender, and religious differences. An evangelizing Church must cultivate *samaritanidad* if it is to effectively engage the diverse cultures of secular humanism and non-Christian religions.

Pastoral Consequences of Pope Francis's Vision

The limits of this presentation do not allow anywhere near a full airing of the pastoral implications of the reforms, the *pastoral conversion*, Pope Francis is proposing for the Church at all levels. By way of conclusion, however, a few obvious points can be made. A candid statement of Archbishop Socrates B. Villegas, president of the Philippine Bishops' Conference, captures the bold nature of the changes the Holy Father has initiated: "Pope Francis has slowly moved the Church from being a dogmatic, self-engrossed, and authoritative sick institution to being a gentle, outreaching, compassionate, and persuasive Church through the power of love and mercy."[18]

The following points capture some of the inspiration and pathos behind specific pastoral consequences of the reform underway as described by Archbishop Villegas. Here a few of those consequences are spelled out:

- A challenge to change the attitudes of bishops, priests, deacons, religious, and lay leaders so that they think as much about those who are not at Mass, who are not currently supporting the parish or are otherwise considered marginal, as they do about the relative few who are active.

- The diocese, parish, Catholic organization, school, or the religious congregation must go beyond its "usual suspects" in order to reach out in the name of Christ, especially to the most marginal and poor. The pope takes the notion of *Evangelii nuntiandi* very seriously: the Church is meant to be entirely missionary. Structures and programs must be evaluated not so much from the point of view of maintenance, as is usually the case, but from that of mission.

- Similarly, every office in the Church from bishop to lector must be viewed not as function or niche but as a sacred missionary calling. Anything that smacks of clericalism, of relegating leadership and

---

18. Archbishop Socrates B. Villegas, address to Philippine Bishops' Conference, July 4, 2014. See CBCP News, "Pope Francis' Papacy 'Biggest Challenge' to PH Church."

- Catechesis must be revised to reflect the dialogical and experiential orientation needed for achieving the encounter with Jesus Christ, which is foremost—a matter of the heart, an affective event more than a rational/cognitive one. Consequently, the role of apologetics and neo-apologetics must be reviewed in terms of the need to stress the kerygmatic and dialogical more than the apologetic and dogmatic in the day-to-day life of the Church.

- Implicit in the turn to the poor, the marginal, as constitutive of Jesus's way of proceeding is the need to move beyond an Enlightenment mindset that fails to see how God is already present in the minds and hearts of the people, especially the poor and even those who lack formal religious formation. This involves realizing that everyone can discover or encounter Christ in the poor.

- As is clearly seen in the specific issues of pastoral concern raised by Pope Francis, the Church's practice must reflect a loving and realistic understanding of people's lives. Hence something must happen to better address the reality of divorced and remarried Catholics, of people who struggle with issues of sexual orientation, of lack of access to the Eucharist due to the shortage of priests, and of issues regarding priestly celibacy.

- A sound pastoral practice requires that disagreements or conflicts within the Church regarding certain teachings and ways to proceed in matters of pastoral care must not be swept under the rug but rather put on the table for fraternal analysis and discussion. This is the path Pope Francis has followed, for example, in the preparations for the October 2014 Synod on the Family. An important feature of the preparation has been the broad consultation with the People of God for the first time ever at the level of the Synod regarding the reality of family and marriage today. This sets an important precedent for serious pastoral planning.

- It goes without saying that Pope Francis's reform urgently requires comprehensive rethinking of seminary formation that takes to heart the renewal he is proposing for all the faithful but especially for the shepherds whose attitudes and way of thinking must reflect those of

service to a chosen few, an elite, is an offense against the Church's very identity and mission, which is thoroughly missionary.

servants not managers, thus giving a more convincing witness to the humility and joy of the Risen Christ.

This is the humility and joy at the heart of the surprising and even astonishing renewal the worldwide Church is undergoing today in the spirit of the Second Vatican Council under the extraordinary leadership of Pope Francis, a conversion firmly grounded in the Gospel itself and in Jorge Mario Bergoglio's deep Latin American and Jesuit roots.

5

Pope Francis and Ignatian Discernment

Peter J. Bernardi, SJ

Next week marks the first anniversary of an unprecedented papal event in the modern era! On February 11, 2013, Pope Benedict XVI made the startling declaration that he intended to "renounce the ministry of the bishop of Rome," effective the evening of February 28, 2013. Before an assembly of ecclesiastics, gathered for the official announcement of some scheduled canonizations, Benedict unexpectedly read in Latin a *declaratio*, written in his own hand, explaining in a firm, calm voice, the reasons for his decision, made "with full freedom," and "after having repeatedly examined [his] conscience before God."[1] He cited as reasons his deteriorating strength and the mental demands of the papacy. Benedict became the first pope in history to resign for reasons of infirmity due to aging.

Benedict's resignation and its context made possible the election of Jorge Mario Bergoglio as the bishop of Rome, on March 13, 2013. This event was also anomalous: the first pope from the Americas; the first pope from the Southern hemisphere (from the "ends of the earth," as he memorably put it), the global South where approximately two-thirds of the world's Roman Catholics now reside. And the unprecedented choice of the name "Francis." Excepting the combined papal name of "John Paul," not

---

1. Glatz and Wooden, "Citing Health Reasons."

since the early tenth century has the bishop of Rome chosen a name not held by a predecessor.[2]

And Francis is the first Jesuit to be elected pope! In the long history of the papacy, only thirty-three vowed religious have been elected bishop of Rome: the first was the monk known to history as St. Gregory the Great (pope, 590–604); and the most recent, before Bergoglio, was the Camaldolese monk Bartolomeo Cappellari, who served as Pope Gregory XVI from 1831 to 1846.

On an ironic note, the Franciscan friar Giovanni Ganganelli, who became Clement XIV (pope, 1769–74), bowing to pressure from European rulers, suppressed the Jesuit order in 1773. But the Benedictine Luigi Chiaramonti, who became Pius VII (pope, 1800–1823), restored the order in 1814. In October 2014, there will be a major academic conference to commemorate this anniversary at Loyola University of Chicago!

The modest aim of my presentation is to highlight some aspects of Ignatian spirituality using the words and actions of Pope Francis. Of course, what characterizes Ignatian spirituality is part of the Church's spiritual patrimony and one need not be a Jesuit to be influenced by it. Furthermore, it would be fatuous to claim that the Ignatian Exercises are the only way these graces can be experienced. Nevertheless, there is a distinctive Ignatian spirituality discernible in the ministry of Pope Francis.

During the return flight to Rome from World Youth Day held in Brazil in the summer of 2013, Francis told reporters, "I feel a Jesuit in my spirituality; in the spirituality of the Exercises, the spirituality deep in my heart. I feel this so deeply that in three days I will go to celebrate with the Jesuits the feast of Saint Ignatius: I will say the morning Mass. I have not changed my spirituality, no. Francis, Franciscan, no. I feel a Jesuit and I think as a Jesuit. I don't mean that hypocritically, but I think as a Jesuit."[3]

For those unfamiliar with the formation a Jesuit receives, let's quickly review the formation of Jorge Mario Bergoglio:

- 1936   Born in Flores, Buenos Aires, to Italian immigrant parents.
- 1950   Starts six-year vocational course at the Escuela Nacional de Educación Técnica leading to a diploma as a chemical technician.

---

2. Lando (pope, 913–14) opted to keep his given name.
3. "Full Transcript of Pope's In-Flight Press Remarks Released."

- 1953   Recognizes vocation during sacrament of confession on September 21.
- 1957   Nearly dies from lung infection.
- 1958   Enters the Jesuit novitiate on March 11.
- 1960   Takes first vows as a Jesuit; studies humanities in Chile.
- 1961–63   Two years of philosophy studies in San Miguel Seminary, Buenos Aires.
- 1964–65   Teaches high school literature and psychology in Colegio de la Inmaculada Concepción in Santa Fe.
- 1966   Teaches in Colegio del Salvador secondary school in Buenos Aires.
- 1967–70   Studies theology at San Miguel Seminary.
- 1969   Ordained to the priesthood on December 13.
- 1970–71   Makes tertianship (final stage of Jesuit formation) at University of Alcalá de Henares in Spain.
- 1971–73   Serves as novice master and vice chancellor, San Miguel Seminary.
- 1973   Takes final vows as a Jesuit on April 22; becomes provincial on July 31.
- 1973–79   Serves as provincial superior of the Jesuits in Argentina and Uruguay.
- 1979–85   Serves as rector of the Colegio Máximo and theology teacher.
- 1986   Spends six months in Germany researching thesis on Romano Guardini; returns to Argentina to teach and serve as confessor of the community of Colegio del Salvador of Buenos Aires, 1986–90.
- 1990–92   Pastoral work at Córdoba.
- 1992   Ordained to the episcopate; becomes auxiliary bishop of Buenos Aires.
- 1997   Appointed coadjutor archbishop of Buenos Aires.
- 1998   Installed as archbishop of Buenos Aires.

- 2001   Made a cardinal by Pope John Paul II; appointed relator at the Synod of Bishops in Rome.
- 2005   Attends papal conclave that elects Pope Benedict.
- 2005–11   Serves as president of the Argentine Bishops' Conference.
- 2007   Chairs the redaction committee of the Final Document of the CELAM Aparecida conference.
- 2013   Elected bishop of Rome on March 13.

Having studied and worked as a chemical technician (and moonlighting as a bouncer!), at the age of twenty-one Jorge Mario entered the Jesuit novitiate. Among the holy desires that attracted him to the Society of Jesus was becoming a missionary to Japan, but the Holy Spirit had other missions in mind! As part of his formation, like every Jesuit, he made two intensive thirty-day "long" retreats based on the Spiritual Exercises of St. Ignatius of Loyola: the first time as a novice, before he took his first vows in 1960; the second time as a "tertian," after having completed a combined seven years of studies in the humanities, philosophy, and theology, and having taught for three years, and after having been ordained to the priesthood in 1969. "Tertianship" is the six- to nine-month program that completes the formal training of a Jesuit. Following the completion of tertianship, a Jesuit awaits an invitation to take final vows, fulfilling a promise he made before God when he took his first vows as a novice. Jorge Mario made his final vows in 1973, just a few months before he was named the provincial superior of the Jesuits in Argentina and Uruguay at the unusually young age of thirty-six.

Besides his six-year term as provincial superior, Bergoglio also served as a "formator" of young Jesuits, first as novice master, when he directed many young Jesuits in the long retreat. Serving as a "formator" requires a deeper level of familiarity with Ignatian spirituality and skill in "discernment of spirits," the ability to distinguish the movements of the good spirit from those of the evil one. Ignatian spirituality is based on St. Ignatius of Loyola's own intense experiences of prayer during his stay at Manresa, Spain, when God led him, "like a patient teacher," to grow in faith and freedom. Ignatius subsequently compiled these exercises in a spiritual handbook, including instructions for directors, in order to help others. They are an ordered series of meditations and contemplations grounded in Scripture that draw the retreatant into a profound encounter with Christ. The retreatant prays to experience a *conocimiento interno*, a deep "interior knowledge" of the "heart of Christ."[4] St. Ignatius wrote, "It is not abundance of knowledge that fills and satisfies the soul, but the inward sense and taste of things!"[5]

The Spiritual Exercises of St. Ignatius of Loyola

The full Exercises have a "four-week" structure: the first week is devoted to the consideration of sin and the overwhelming Mercy of God; the second week focuses on the life of Christ as far as Palm Sunday inclusive; the third week meditates on the Passion and death of Christ; and the fourth on His Resurrection and Ascension. The graced fruits of making the Exercises include remorse for one's sin; a transformative experience of God's loving mercy; reverence for creation; humility and prudence, fidelity and compassion, joy and gratitude; and overall a spiritual freedom that enables one to respond to the Lord with generous, loving deeds.[6]

The trademark of Ignatian spirituality is "find[ing] God in all things." Ignatian principles of discernment enable a person to recognize the genuine movements of God's Spirit as well as the capacity to detect the spirit of the evil one, who sometimes masquerades as an "angel of light."

In the widely publicized interview with Fr. Antonio Spadaro, SJ, editor of *La Civiltà Cattolica*, Pope Francis remarked,

> Discernment is one of the things that worked inside St. Ignatius. For him it is an instrument of struggle in order to know the Lord and follow him more closely. I was always struck by a saying that describes the vision of Ignatius: *non coerceri a maximo, sed contineri a minimo divinum est* ("not to be limited by the greatest and yet to be contained in the tiniest—this is the divine"). I thought a lot about this phrase in connection with the issue of different roles in the government of the church, about becoming the superior of somebody else: it is important not to be restricted by a larger space, and it is important to be able to stay in restricted spaces. This virtue of the large and small is magnanimity. Thanks to magnanimity, we can always look at the horizon from the position where we are. That means being able to do the little things of every day with a big heart open to God and to others. That means being

---

4. See Fagin, *Putting on the Heart of Christ*.
5. Ignatius, *Spiritual Exercises*, Annotations, no. 2.
6. Fagin, *Putting on the Heart of Christ*, passim.

able to appreciate the small things inside large horizons, those of the kingdom of God.[7]

He continued:

> This motto offers parameters to assume a correct position for discernment, in order to hear the things of God from God's "point of view." According to St. Ignatius, great principles must be embodied in the circumstances of place, time and people . . .
>
> This discernment takes time. For example, many think that changes and reforms can take place in a short time. I believe that we always need time to lay the foundations for real, effective change. And this is the time of discernment. Sometimes discernment instead urges us to do precisely what you had at first thought you would do later. And that is what has happened to me in recent months. Discernment is always done in the presence of the Lord, looking at the signs, listening to the things that happen, the feeling of the people, especially the poor. My choices, including those related to the day-to-day aspects of life, like the use of a modest car, are related to a spiritual discernment that responds to a need that arises from looking at things, at people and from reading the signs of the times. Discernment in the Lord guides me in my way of governing.
>
> But I am always wary of decisions made hastily. I am always wary of the first decision, that is, the first thing that comes to my mind if I have to make a decision. This is usually the wrong thing. I have to wait and assess, looking deep into myself, taking the necessary time. The wisdom of discernment redeems the necessary ambiguity of life and helps us find the most appropriate means, which do not always coincide with what looks great and strong.
>
> Finding God in all things is not an "empirical *eureka*." When we desire to encounter God, we would like to verify him immediately by an empirical method. But you cannot meet God this way. God is found in the gentle breeze perceived by Elijah. The senses that find God are the ones St. Ignatius called spiritual senses. Ignatius asks us to open our spiritual sensitivity to encounter God beyond a purely empirical approach. A contemplative attitude is necessary: it is the feeling that you are moving along the good path of understanding and affection toward things and situations. Profound peace, spiritual consolation, love of God and love of all things in God—this is the sign that you are on this right path.[8]

7. Spadaro, "A Big Heart Open to God," 17.
8. Ibid., 30.

Pope Francis was asked, "So if the encounter with God is not an 'empirical *eureka*,' and if it is a journey that sees with the eyes of history, then we can also make mistakes?" He replied,

> Yes, in this quest to seek and find God in all things there is still an area of uncertainty. There must be. If a person says that he met God with total certainty and is not touched by a margin of uncertainty, then this is not good. For me, this is an important key. If one has the answers to all the questions—that is the proof that God is not with him. It means that he is a false prophet using religion for himself. The great leaders of the people of God, like Moses, have always left room for doubt. You must leave room for the Lord, not for our certainties; we must be humble. Uncertainty is in every true discernment that is open to finding confirmation in spiritual consolation.
>
> The risk in seeking and finding God in all things, then, is the willingness to explain too much, to say with human certainty and arrogance: "God is here." We will find only a god that fits our measure. The correct attitude is that of St. Augustine: seek God to find him, and find God to keep searching for God forever . . . We must enter into the adventure of the quest for meeting God; we must let God search and encounter us.
>
> Because God is first; God is always first and makes the first move . . . We read it in the Prophets. God is encountered walking, along the path. At this juncture, someone might say that this is relativism. Is it relativism? Yes, if it is misunderstood as a kind of indistinct pantheism. It is not relativism if it is understood in the biblical sense, that God is always a surprise, so you never know where and how you will find him. You are not setting the time and place of the encounter with him. You must, therefore, discern the encounter. Discernment is essential.[9]

On the return flight from Brazil, Francis offered an example of how discernment had led him to change his mind:

> You asked about the Charismatic Renewal movement. I'll tell you one thing. Back at the end of the 1970s and the beginning of the 1980s, I had no time for them. Once, speaking about them, I said: "These people confuse a liturgical celebration with samba lessons!" I actually said that. Now I regret it. I learned. It is also true that the movement, with good leaders, has made great progress. Now I think that this movement does much good for the Church,

9. Ibid., 30, 32.

> overall. In Buenos Aires, I met frequently with them and once a year I celebrated a Mass with all of them in the Cathedral. I have always supported them, after I was *converted*, after I saw the good they were doing.[10]

This illustrates the classic principle of discernment articulated by Jesus: "You shall know them by their fruits."

The practice of discernment entails "listening," which is a prominent theme in Francis's utterances, especially his apostolic exhortation *Evangelii gaudium*. Listening entails respect for the mystery of God's grace at work in people's lives, an attentive openness to human experience. In his address to the leaders of religious congregations in December 2013, the pope spoke of "the need to become acquainted with reality by experience, to spend time walking on the periphery in order really to become acquainted with the reality and life experiences of people. If this does not happen we then run the risk of being abstract ideologists or fundamentalists, which is not healthy."[11]

And in the Spadaro interview, he said, "I have a dogmatic certainty: God is in every person's life. God is in everyone's life. Even if the life of a person has been a disaster, even if it is destroyed by vices, drugs or anything else—God is in this person's life. You can, you must try to seek God in every human life. Although the life of a person is a land full of thorns and weeds, there is always a space in which the good seed can grow. You have to trust God."[12] I detect here an echo of the theology of grace of Jesuit theologian Karl Rahner (1904–84), who played such an important role at Vatican II. The year 2014 marks the thirtieth anniversary of Rahner's death (March 30, 1984).

On various occasions, Francis has expressed respect for persons and their concrete spiritual experience. In the "Wake Up the World" reflections about religious life, recorded by Spadaro, Francis said, "In the end I cannot form a person as a religious without consideration of his or her life, experience, mentality and cultural context. This is the way to proceed. This is what the great missionaries did."[13]

Notably, when asked about homosexual persons, Francis responded, "We must always consider the person. Here we enter into the mystery of the human being. In life, God accompanies persons, and we must accompany

---

10. "Full Transcript of Pope's In-Flight Press Remarks Released."
11. Spadaro, "Wake Up the World," 4.
12. Spadaro, "A Big Heart Open to God," 32.
13. Spadaro, "Wake Up the World," 7.

them, starting from their situation. It is necessary to accompany them with mercy. When that happens, the Holy Spirit inspires the priest to say the right thing."[14]

As archbishop of Buenos Aires, Cardinal Jorge Bergoglio had played a major role in preparing the Final Report of the Fifth Latin American and Caribbean Bishops' Conference that met in 2007 in Aparecida, Brazil. This document expressed these same concerns: "Personal conversion engenders the ability to make everything subject to establishing the Kingdom of life. We bishops, priests, permanent deacons, religious men and women, and lay men and women are called to assume an attitude of ongoing pastoral conversion, which entails listening attentively and discerning 'what the Spirit says to the churches' (Rev 2:29) through the signs of the times in which God is made manifest."[15]

Pope Francis's apostolic exhortation *Evangelii gaudium* reiterated these themes:

> A Church which "goes forth" is a Church whose doors are open. Going out to others in order to reach the fringes of humanity does not mean rushing out aimlessly into the world. Often it is better simply to slow down, to put aside our eagerness in order to see and listen to others, to stop rushing from one thing to another and to remain with someone who has faltered along the way. At times we have to be like the father of the prodigal son, who always keeps his door open so that when the son returns, he can readily pass through it.[16]

Because the pope wants a "humble, listening, discerning Church," he calls for a reform of consultative and collegial structures in the Church.[17]

> I prefer a Church which is bruised, hurting and dirty because it has been out on the streets, rather than a Church which is unhealthy from being confined and from clinging to its own security. I do not want a Church concerned with being at the center and which then ends by being caught up in a web of obsessions and procedures. If something should rightly disturb us and trouble our consciences, it is the fact that so many of our brothers and sisters are living without the strength, light and consolation born

---

14. Spadaro, "A Big Heart Open to God," 26.
15. CELAM, *Concluding Document: Aparecida*, no. 366.
16. Pope Francis, *Evangelii gaudium*, 46.
17. Gaillardetz, "Francis Wishes to Release Vatican II's Bold Vision."

of friendship with Jesus Christ, without a community of faith to support them, without meaning and a goal in life. More than by fear of going astray, my hope is that we will be moved by the fear of remaining shut up within structures which give us a false sense of security, within rules which make us harsh judges, within habits which make us feel safe, while at our door people are starving and Jesus does not tire of saying to us: "Give them something to eat" (Mark 6:37).[18]

And during World Youth Day, he said, "I want the Church to be in the streets; I want us to defend ourselves against all that is worldliness, comfort, being closed and turned within. Parishes, colleges, and institutions must get out, otherwise they risk becoming NGOs, and the Church is not a NGO [i.e., nongovernmental organization]."[19]

There is much in Francis's writings and interviews that reflects the First Week of the Ignatian Exercises. On more than one occasion, he has acknowledged his own sinfulness and his heartfelt experience of God's *mercy*. Indeed, God's overwhelming Mercy is a persistent theme in his preaching.

When Spadaro asked him, "Who is Jorge Mario Bergoglio?" the pope responded, "I am a sinner. This is the most accurate definition. It is not a figure of speech, a literary genre. I am a sinner ... Yes, perhaps I can say that I am a bit astute, that I can adapt to circumstances, but it is also true that I am a bit naïve. Yes, but the best summary, the one that comes more from the inside and I feel most true is this: I am a sinner whom the Lord has looked upon." And he reiterated, "I am one who is looked upon by the Lord. I always felt my motto, *Miserando atque Eligendo* [By Having Mercy and by Choosing Him], was very true for me."[20]

In the years before his election as bishop of Rome, Bergoglio often visited the Church of St. Louis of France in Rome to contemplate *The Calling of St. Matthew*, by Caravaggio. "That finger of Jesus, pointing at Matthew. That's me. I feel like him. Like Matthew ... It is the gesture of Matthew that strikes me: he holds on to his money as if to say, 'No, not me! No, this money is mine.' Here, this is me, a sinner on whom the Lord has turned his gaze. And this is what I said when they asked me if I would accept my election as pontiff." Then the pope whisper[ed] in Latin: "I am a sinner, but

---

18. Pope Francis, *Evangelii gaudium*, 49.
19. "Pope Francis to the Youth and to the Aged."
20. Spadaro, "A Big Heart Open to God," 16.

I trust in the infinite mercy and patience of our Lord Jesus Christ, and I accept in a spirit of penance."[21]

In fact, it was on the Feast of Saint Matthew, in 1953, that the seventeen-year-old Jorge Mario Bergoglio experienced a call to priesthood when receiving the Sacrament of Penance. He recalled more than fifty years later, "Something strange happened to me in that confession. I don't know what it was, but it changed my life. I think it surprised me, caught me with my guard down . . . It was the surprise, the astonishment of a chance encounter . . . This is the religious experience: the astonishment of meeting someone who has been waiting for you all along. From that moment on, for me, God is the One who *te primerea*—'springs it on you.' You search for Him, but He searches for you first. You want to find Him, but He finds you first."[22]

At the end of the First Week of the Spiritual Exercises, there is a meditation titled "The Call of the King," which concludes with a Triple Prayer Colloquy. Francis has remarked, "For me it is the memory of which St. Ignatius speaks in the First Week of the Exercises in the encounter with the merciful Christ crucified. And I ask myself: 'What have I done for Christ? What am I doing for Christ? What should I do for Christ?'"[23] "The Call of the King" meditation serves as a segue into the Second Week of the Spiritual Exercises that brings the retreatant into a "*Personal encounter with the saving love of Jesus.*"[24] While not unique to Francis, he repeatedly focuses on the loving "gaze," both the Lord's merciful gaze fixed on us and the exhortation for us to "gaze" on Christ, especially the crucified Christ, who has emptied himself on our behalf. The "gaze" is a concrete expression of the saving, transformative "encounter" with the Lord that is frequently emphasized in the Final "Aparecida" Report (ninety-three times) and in Francis's Apostolic Exhortation *Evangelii gaudium* (thirty-four times). This encounter is foundational for the "missionary disciple."

"Knowing Jesus is the best gift that any person can receive; that we have encountered Him is the best thing that has happened in our lives, and making him known by our word and deeds is our joy."[25]

---

21. Ibid. For a short presentation on this painting, see http://www.youtube.com/watch?v=RtnIkvsWTIw.

22. Rubin and Ambrogetti, *Pope Francis*, 34.

23. Spadaro, "A Big Heart Open to God," 38.

24. Pope Francis, *Evangelii gaudium*, 264.

25. *Concluding Document: Aparecida*, no. 29.

Authentic encounter with Christ energizes his disciples for mission. Francis, it seems to me, often has in mind, even if the term is unspoken, the Ignatian *magis* (Latin for "more"), namely, an appeal to bold generosity on behalf of God's Kingdom. Francis exhorts the People of God, in virtue of their baptismal vocation, to be "missionary disciples," not to be afraid to go to the "peripheries," literally and figuratively, to make contact with the excluded, the alienated, and the marginalized. His pastoral ministry has exemplified many ways to encounter Christ in the poor and the excluded, to be with Christ at the margins, the periphery, the frontiers. Especially moving was the embrace he gave to Vinicio Riva, who has suffered horrifically from neurofibromatosis since he was fifteen years old.

> An evangelizing community gets involved by word and deed in people's daily lives; it bridges distances, it is willing to abase itself if necessary, and it embraces human life, touching the suffering flesh of Christ in others. Evangelizers thus take on the "smell of the sheep" and the sheep are willing to hear their voice.[26]

Francis imagines the Church as a "field hospital" that is present to people who are suffering and estranged. He criticizes viewing the Church as a secure enclave, safe from the contagion of the world. In Buenos Aires, Archbishop Bergoglio regularly visited the poorest neighborhoods, *villas de miserias*, both to get to know the poor and to encourage the priests who were missioned to live with the poor. The number of priests and seminarians who lived and worked with the poor doubled during his years as archbishop. He wrote in his apostolic exhortation, "There is one sign which we should never lack: the option for those who are least, those whom society discards."[27] But going to the "periphery" also includes dialogue with those alienated from Christian faith, such as when the pope took the initiative to meet with the atheistic editor of *La Repubblica*, Eugenio Scalfiari.[28]

The Second Week of the Spiritual Exercises features two meditations that have deeply influenced Francis. In the "Two Standards Meditation," the retreatant prays for the grace to understand and embrace the strategy of Christ, which is diametrically opposed to the insidious temptations of the evil one, the enemy of our nature. It is the stratagem of the evil one to tempt people with riches, then to vain honors, and finally to the state of "swollen pride." In contrast, the strategy of Christ is first to draw people "to the

---

26. Pope Francis, *Evangelii gaudium*, 24.
27. Ibid., 195.
28. See Scalfari, "The Pope," but also see Gagliarducci, "Pope's Words."

highest spiritual poverty," and if the Lord wills to choose them, "not less to actual poverty"; secondly, "to desire reproaches and affronts, because from these experiences comes humility. In sum, the strategy of Christ embraces poverty, not riches; insults and humiliations, not worldly honors; and humility, not egocentric pride; by these three stages, the disciples of Christ are to be led to all the other virtues."[29] The meditation on the "Consideration of the Three Modes of Humility" similarly highlights the "third" degree of humility, which is to desire and choose poverty with Christ rather than riches; to experience insults with Christ rather than worldly honors; and finally, "to be accounted a good-for-nothing and a fool for Christ's sake rather than to be accounted a worldly success."[30] Gerry Fagin conveys the gist of these meditations: "Christ calls us to simplicity, poverty of spirit, selflessness, sharing, compassion, cooperation, concern for others, community, inclusion, and solidarity with the poor. In contrast, Satan calls us to consumerism, competition, narcissism, individualism, exclusion, and suspicion of others."[31]

In one of his "morning meditations" given in the chapel of Casa Santa Marta, where he resides, Pope Francis expressed the graces of these meditations: "The sign that 'a Christian is a true Christian' is his ability to bear humiliation with joy and patience . . . [to] look upon the Lord and ask for humiliation in order to be more closely conformed to him."[32] The humility and simplicity of Francis have touched people well beyond the Church's membership!

In contrast with the strategy of Christ are the deceptions of the evil one. Francis has repeatedly expressed the need to guard against the temptation to "spiritual worldliness," a phrase taken from Jesuit theologian Henri de Lubac's work *Splendour of the Church*.[33] In an address to the priests after the Aparecida meeting in 2008, Archbishop Bergoglio highlighted the special capacity of the People of God to sniff out pastors who have been corrupted:

> The faithful People of God, to whom we belong, from which we learned and to whom we are sent, has a special sense of smell,

29. Ignatius, *Spiritual Exercises*, no. 146.
30. Ibid., no. 167.
31. Fagin, *Putting on the Heart of Christ*, 103.
32. Pope Francis, "On the Path of Jesus."
33. See de Lubac, *Splendour of the Church*, 377–78. The Spanish word for "worldly," *mundano*, is found in the Two Standards Meditation.

which comes from the *sensus fidei*, to recognize when a shepherd of the people is turning into a cleric of the State, into a bureaucrat [*funzionario*]. It is not the same case as a priest sinner, [which] we all are, and we remain in the flock. Instead, the worldly priest enters in a different process, a process—the term comes to mind—of spiritual corruption—that attacks the spiritual nature itself of the shepherd, perverts it and gives him a status different from the holy People of God. Both the prophet Ezekiel and St. Augustine in his Sermon 46 *De Pastoribus* identify this type of shepherd with the one who takes advantage of the flock; he takes the milk and the wool. Aparecida, throughout its message to priests, aims at the genuine identity of the "shepherd of the people," and not that of an adulterated "cleric of the State."[34]

This perspective informed Cardinal Bergoglio's address to the cardinals before the conclave that resulted in his election as the bishop of Rome. His dynamic missionary vision of the Church, not obsessed with her own security, is said to have galvanized the cardinals.[35]

We have to avoid the spiritual sickness of a self-referential church. It's true that when you get out into the street, as happens to every man and woman, there can be accidents. However, if the church remains closed in on itself, self-referential, it gets old. Between a church that suffers accidents in the street, and a church that's sick because it's self-referential, I have no doubts about preferring the former.[36]

In response to the pervasive ecclesial "desolation" resulting from well-publicized scandals and curial infighting that threatened to impede the action of the evangelizing Spirit, Bergoglio effectively applied St. Ignatius's rules of discernment.[37] The spiritual strategy in such circumstances is "to go against" (*agere contra*) the temptation to self-preoccupation. What is needed is for the Church to recover its missionary élan! This inspiring vision evidently struck a nerve with the cardinal electors.

The Third and Fourth Weeks of the Spiritual Exercises focus on the death and resurrection of Christ, respectively. The grace of the Third Week

---

34. Bergoglio, "Il messaggio."

35. "The church on earth is by its very nature missionary . . ." See Vatican Council II, *Decree Ad Gentes*, 2.

36. "Havana Prelate Shares Notes."

37. See Ignatius, *Spiritual Exercises*, nos. 313–36. I am grateful to Bill Creed, SJ, for this insight.

is epitomized in the experience of St. Ignatius in a chapel at La Storta, then on the outskirts of Rome. Ignatius saw Christ carrying his cross and heard a heavenly voice: "Take this man to labor with you." Ignatius received confirmation of his desire to labor at the side of the Son under the standard of the cross, which is a "standard of poverty and humility and self-abdication."[38]

Joy is the special grace of the Fourth Week: "The Resurrection of Jesus is the source of our joy, our peace, and our hope."[39] Needless to say, *joy* is patent in Francis's ministry! And joy is a central theme in his apostolic exhortation!

The Ignatian Exercises conclude with "The Contemplation to Attain Love."[40] The retreatant is asked to consider "how all good things and gifts descend from above, as my limited powers from that power sovereign and infinite above, and so justice, goodness, pity, mercy, etc., as from the sun come down the rays, from the spring the waters, etc."[41] This contemplation relates to Ignatius's Cardoner River experience. In his "Autobiography," he recalled, "He [Ignatius] sat down for a little while with his face to the river which was running deep. While he was seated there, the eyes of his understanding began to be opened; though he did not see any vision, he understood and knew many things, both spiritual things and matters of faith and learning, and this was with so great an enlightenment that everything seemed new to him . . . After this had lasted for a good while, he went to kneel before a nearby cross to give thanks to God."[42] In the Spadaro interview, Francis said,

> Prayer for me is always a prayer full of memory, of recollection, even the memory of my own history or what the Lord has done in his church or in a particular parish . . . It is the memory of which Ignatius speaks in the "Contemplation for Experiencing [Attaining] Divine Love," when he asks us to recall the gifts we have received. But above all, I also know that the Lord remembers me. I can forget about him, but I know that he never, ever forgets me. Memory has a fundamental role for the heart of a Jesuit: memory of grace, the memory mentioned in Deuteronomy, the memory of God's works that are the basis of the covenant between God

---

38. Fagin, *Putting on the Heart of Christ*, 78.
39. Ibid., 197.
40. Ignatius, *Spiritual Exercises*, nos. 230–37.
41. Ibid., no. 237.
42. Ignatius, *Autobiography*, 39–40.

and the people. It is this memory that makes me his son and that makes me a father, too.[43]

As Francis succinctly expressed in his apostolic exhortation, "The believer is essentially 'one who remembers'" with gratitude.[44]

Conclusion

Since becoming the bishop of Rome, Francis's Jesuit formation has surely influenced a special papal act, namely, the "equivalent" canonization of Peter Favre (1506–46), one of St. Ignatius's first companions and a founding member of the Society of Jesus.[45] Echoing Jesuit scholar Michel de Certeau, Francis considers Favre the model of the "reformed" priest. The pope admires "[Peter Favre's] dialogue with all . . . even the most remote and even with his opponents; his simple piety, a certain naïveté perhaps, his being available straightaway, his careful interior discernment, the fact that he was a man capable of great and strong decisions but also capable of being so gentle and loving."[46] And in his homily for the feast of the Most Holy Name of Jesus at the Church of the Gesù in Rome, Francis held up Favre "as an apostolic model, a person of great desires, with a holy 'restlessness' for the sake of Christ's Kingdom" who united an 'exquisite' sensibility with the capacity to make decisions."[47] The pope cited from Favre's autobiographical *Memoriale*: "That the first movement of the heart must be that of 'desiring what is essential and original, that is, that the first place be left to the perfect solicitude of finding God our Lord' [no. 63]; Favre demonstrates the desire 'to let Christ occupy the center of our heart' [no. 68]."[48] Francis added, "Only if one is centered on God is it possible to go to the fringes of the world! . . . Favre was devoured by the intense desire to communicate the Lord. If we do not have this same desire, then we need to pause in prayer

---

43. Spadaro, "A Big Heart Open to God," 38.

44. Pope Francis, *Evangelii gaudium*, 13.

45. The canonization was announced on December 17, 2013. An "equivalent" canonization means that the requirement of a second miracle was waived. This was also the case with the canonization of Hildegard of Bingen by Pope Benedict and of Pope John XXIII by Pope Francis. See "Pope Francis Declares Sainthood of Early Jesuit."

46. Spadaro, "A Big Heart Open to God," 20.

47. See "Pope Francis' Homily at Mass."

48. See ibid. The numbers in brackets refer to the section numbers of Favre's *Memoriale*.

and, with silent fervor, ask the Lord, through the intercession of our brother Peter, that he fascinate us again: that fascination of the Lord that led Peter to all his apostolic 'lunacies.'"[49] As St. Peter Favre wrote, "We never seek in this life a name that is not connected with that of Jesus" (no. 205). I think that this is the key to understanding Francis's Petrine ministry.

---

49. See "Pope Francis' Homily at Mass."

6

Pope Francis, the Ecclesial Movements, and the New Evangelization

Ann W. Astell

When Jorge Bergoglio, archbishop of Buenos Aires, was elected pope on March 11, 2013, media reports frequently mentioned his affiliation with the Communion and Liberation (CL) Movement founded by Luigi Giussani (1922–2005).[1] While the degree of his ties to CL was perhaps somewhat exaggerated in the reports, Communion and Liberation has indeed affected Bergoglio's spirituality and his vision of an evangelizing Church. Indeed, Archbishop Bergoglio's experience of Communion and Liberation and of other important ecclesial movements, both in South America and in Italy, has helped prepare him as pope to call the whole Church to announce to a needy world the joy of the Gospel, *evangelii gaudium*.[2]

Using the papal relationship to the ecclesial movements as a touchstone, I argue that Pope Francis's own view of them reveals not only a striking continuity with his predecessors, John Paul II and Benedict XVI, but also a development. The continuity between and among the three popes can easily be seen by noting briefly each of their respective meetings with members of the ecclesial movements in Rome—large-scale encounters in 1998, 2006, and 2013, each of them connected significantly with the feast

---

1. See Manson, "One of Pope Francis' Allegiances." Manson cites a report by the Vatican journalist John Allen, who claimed that the Argentine cardinal "became close to the *Comunione e liberazione* movement over the years."

2. Pope Francis, *Evangelii gaudium*.

of Pentecost. The development from Pope John Paul II to Pope Francis becomes visible in two ways: first, the degree to which Pope Francis not only recognizes, supports, and blesses but also participates personally in these movements; second, the striking coincidence between Francis's missionary impulse and exhortation, on the one hand, and the evangelizing practices and proven effectiveness of the movements, on the other. If contemplating the life and history of the movements led Pope John Paul II to name "the Church herself . . . a movement and . . . a mystery,"[3] Pope Francis seeks to animate the Church's earthly pilgrimage toward Christ through her joyful outreach to the poor, the needy, and the alienated—an evangelical outreach that the recognized ecclesial movements have wonderfully exemplified.

On May 30, 1998, at a "truly unprecedented" Pentecostal gathering of more than three hundred thousand movement members in St. Peter's Square in Rome,[4] John Paul II prophetically recognized the activity of the Holy Spirit at work in them as a timely answer to the needs of the Church after Vatican Council II (1962–65). Brendan Leahy has called this papal encounter with the movements "a decisive turning point" in their development within the life of the Church.[5] In *Christifideles laici*, the document that was the fruit of the 1987 Synod of Bishops on the Laity, John Paul II had established five criteria for the discernment of the authenticity of these modern, largely lay movements: (1) "the primacy given to the call of every Christian to holiness," (2) "the responsibility of professing the Catholic faith," (3) "the witness to a strong and authentic communion in filial relationship to the Pope . . . and with the local Bishop," (4) "conformity to and participation in the Church's apostolic goals," and (5) "a commitment to presence in human society . . . in light of the Church's social doctrine."[6] Calling the modern ecclesial movements to a greater ecclesial maturity and integration, Pope John Paul II protected many of them canonically as international associations of the faithful recognized officially by the Pontifical Council for the Laity.[7] In 1998, that same pontiff hailed the rise of these

---

3. John Paul II, "Homily at the Mass for Participants at the Congress of 'Movements in the Church.'"

4. John Paul II, "Meeting with Ecclesial Movements and New Communities."

5. Leahy, *Ecclesial Movements and Communities*, 56.

6. John Paul II, *Christifideles laici*, 30.

7. The Vatican website lists 122 international associations of the faithful. See http://www.vatican.va/roman_curia/pontifical_councils/laity/documents/rc_pc_laity_doc_20051114_associazioni_en.html.

movements as "one of the most significant fruits of that springtime in the Church which was foretold by the Second Vatican Council."[8]

Supporting the initiative of Pope John Paul II, Cardinal Ratzinger brilliantly articulated the theological placement, the *locus*, of the movements within the Church's life and history.[9] In 1999 he engaged bishops from five continents, gathered for an episcopal synod on the movements, in a pastoral dialogue about them.[10] He opened that dialogue with a witness concerning his personal encounters with movement members, starting in the mid-1960s, when he first met a group of Neocatechumens in Tübingen, Germany. In it, he mentions several significant, positive engagements also with Communion and Liberation and the Catholic Charismatic Renewal.[11] Later, as Benedict XVI, he repeated on June 3, 2006, the moving, historic gesture of a papal encounter with hundreds of thousands of movement members in Rome on the vigil of Pentecost.

Francis, too, has shown himself eager to meet with the movements, individually and collectively, welcoming an estimated two hundred thousand movement members to Rome in May 2013, shortly after his elevation to the papal see. This encounter took place at Pentecost and provided Pope Francis with an opportunity to address the movements collectively as agents of the "new evangelization" to which the whole Church is called.[12] Even more than his predecessors, perhaps, Francis discovers in these movements a collective model or mirror *for the Church itself* as a missionary movement of persons and communities chosen in mercy by Christ to be "the light of the world" (Matt 5:14).[13] As Giancarlo Faletti, copresident of the Focolare, has stressed, Pope Francis speaks to the Church as a whole when he addresses the movements.[14] Like the Church as a whole, the movements are to avoid turning in upon themselves; rather, they are to go out to the outsiders, into the city streets, into the workplaces, to proclaim Jesus Christ in word and

---

8. John Paul II, "Message for the World Congress of Ecclesial Movements and New Communities."

9. Ratzinger, "Ecclesial Movements," 17–62.

10. Ratzinger, "The Movements, the Church, the World," 65–117.

11. Ibid., 65–69.

12. Ever since the publication in 1990 of Pope John Paul II's encyclical *Redemptoris missio*, the "new evangelization" has been a motto and a watchword especially for Christian witness in the increasingly secularized milieu of the Western nations.

13. Emphasis mine. For biblical references, I use throughout the New American Bible Revised Edition (Oxford: Oxford University Press, 2011).

14. See "Focolare President Promises Pope Testimony of Joy."

service, especially to the poor. While all three popes (like popes before them) have pointed to Mary as the "great missionary," and theologians—Joseph Ratzinger among them—have followed Hans Urs von Balthasar (1905–88) in associating the movements with the "Marian principle" of the Church,[15] Francis is helping people through his own example and that set by the movements to understand better what a merciful, joyful, Marian style or manner of evangelizing looks like for the whole people of God.

In this essay I proceed in three parts. First, I briefly chronicle Francis's contacts with the movements, before and during his still-young papacy. Second, I focus on Communion and Liberation, looking over Jorge Bergoglio's shoulder in his reading of Luigi Giussani's writings in order to see their significance for him. Finally, I turn to the question of Pope Francis's Mariology in the context of his encounters with the ecclesial movements. Francis's consecration of his papacy to our Lady of Fatima must be understood, I argue, in the light of the Marian principle he sees animating the movements and the Church as a whole in its love for Christ, the Savior of the world.

Pope Francis and the Movements

Following the example set by the two previous popes, Francis gathered with an estimated two hundred thousand movement members, representing 150 different movements, for the celebration of Pentecost in St. Peter's Square on May 19, 2013. He also addressed them on the previous day, the vigil of the feast. Only two months into his papacy, Francis embraced the opportunity to support the evangelical fervor of these largely lay movements, which represent for him a charismatic openness to "newness," to "God's surprises," to a harmonious "variety and diversity," and, above all, to mission.[16] "The Holy Spirit," he told the assembly, "is the soul of *mission* ... It is the Paraclete Spirit, the 'Comforter,' who grants us the courage to take to the streets of the world, bringing the Gospel!"[17]

A highlighting of a few of the largest movements—Catholic Charismatic Renewal, Schoenstatt, Neocatechumenal Way, Focolare, Sant'Egidio, Communion and Liberation, and the Fatima Apostolate—in their

---

15. See Leahy, *Ecclesial Movements and Communities*, 119–25, and Hanna, *New Ecclesial Movements*, 193–213.
16. Pope Francis, "Solemnity of Pentecost."
17. Ibid., 3.

encounters with Francis shows the warmth of the pope's regard for them. Pope Francis stresses the ecclesial purpose of the different charisms operative in these movements in his apostolic exhortation *Evangelii gaudium*. There he writes,

> [The charisms] are not an inheritance, safely secured and entrusted to a small group for safekeeping; rather they are gifts of the Spirit integrated into the body of the Church, drawn to the center which is Christ and then channeled into an evangelizing impulse. A sure sign of the authenticity of a charism is its ecclesial character, its ability to be integrated harmoniously into the life of God's holy and faithful people for the good of all.[18]

Here, Pope Francis employs the language of charism with specific reference to the "small group" of the individual movement, association, or community. Evangelical activity is the remedy Francis prescribes for the spiritual elitism that would mistake a gift for a possession, instead of seeing it as something to be used, shared, put into the service of others. As Leahy points out, "The documents of the Second Vatican Council make fifteen direct references to the notion of charism," and as many as a hundred of the Council's documents "refer to the theme of charism."[19] Indeed, the Council attached special importance to St. Paul's vision of the Church as comprised of many members endowed with different gifts (charisms and charismata) suited to different ministries and thus to the Church's unity in charity as Christ's Mystical Body.[20]

In the years since the Council, all the popes have recognized the ecclesial movements as possessing charisms and challenged them to use their gifts in the service of the Church as a whole. As its name suggests, the Catholic Charismatic Renewal (CCR) has an iconic status among the many movements in this regard, in part because the CCR, unlike other ecclesial movements, does not trace its historical origin to a charismatically gifted human founder or saint, but rather to the direct action of the Holy Spirit.[21] Speaking to the Brazilian TV journalist Marcio Campos on

18. Pope Francis, *Evangelii gaudium*, 130.
19. Leahy, *Ecclesial Movements and Communities*, 88.
20. See chapters 12 and 13 of 1 Corinthians.
21. See Whitehead, *Catholic Charismatic Renewal*, 3: "The Catholic Charismatic Renewal is not a single unified worldwide movement as the others are. It does not have a founder or group of founders as other movements do." See also Hanna, *New Ecclesial Movements*, 77–95.

the plane during the return flight from Rio after World Youth Day, Pope Francis commented in particular on the Catholic Charismatic Renewal: "It renews us." He added, "The movements are necessary, the movements are a grace of the Spirit."[22]

On Saturday, April 27, 2013, Archbishop Rino Fisichella, president of the Pontifical Council for Promoting the New Evangelization, gave an unexpected greeting from Pope Francis to the fifteen thousand Catholic charismatics gathered in Rimini, Italy, for the thirty-sixth national assembly of Catholic Charismatic Renewal. "Tell them," Pope Francis had urged the archbishop, "that I love them very much!" Pope Francis added, by way of explanation, "I was responsible for the Charismatic Renewal in Argentina."[23] Formerly skeptical about the Catholic Charismatic Movement in Latin America, Bergoglio came to respect and appreciate it, not just as a Catholic alternative for those attracted by Protestant Pentecostalism and its prosperity gospel, but "as a service to the Church herself."[24] Reporting a membership of at least 120 million Catholics in 238 countries, the Catholic Charismatic Renewal, which started during a student retreat at Duquesne University in Pittsburgh in 1967, is now strongest in Africa and in Latin America, where "16 percent of Catholics identify themselves as participants."[25]

Hailed by Catholic charismatics worldwide as a "charismatic pope," Francis recently announced that he will attend the thirty-seventh meeting of the Catholic Charismatic Renewal at the Olympic Stadium, in Rome, June 1–2. Although previous popes, beginning in 1975 with Pope Paul VI, have addressed and blessed large gatherings of Catholic charismatics at the Vatican, Francis will be the first pope actually to participate in the meeting of this movement, which was officially approved in 1990 by the Pontifical Council for the Laity as a Catholic Fraternity of Charismatic Covenant Communities and Fellowships. Fifty thousand participants are expected to gather alongside the pope in Rome.

"The Spirit and the bride say, 'Come'" (Rev 22:17). Brazil, famous for its Marian devotion, has been called "the center of gravity of the

---

22. Rocca, "Pope Francis Discovers Charismatic Movement a Gift."
23. García, "Pope to Catholic Charismatic Renewal."
24. Rocca, "Pope Francis Discovers Charismatic Movement a Gift."
25. Ibid. On the growth of the Catholic Charismatic Movement in Latin America, see also Maurer, *Spirit of Enthusiasm*, 58–60.

Latin American CCR," where "at least half of all active Catholics ... are Charismatics."[26] Members of the Catholic Charismatic Renewal and of various explicitly Marian ecclesial movements thronged Pope Francis in Rio de Janiero, Brazil, greeting him with arms upraised and with the picture of our Lady of Schoenstatt. At the explicit and unusual request of Pope Francis, a young Schoenstatt priest, Fr. Alexandre Awi Mello, accompanied the Holy Father throughout his travels in Brazil. An acquaintance of Cardinal Bergoglio since 2007, Fr. Awi, the National Director of the Schoenstatt Movement in Brazil, later met privately in Rome with Pope Francis, who keeps an image of our Lady of Schoenstatt at his bedside.

Founded in Germany in 1914 by Fr. Joseph Kentenich (1885–1968), Schoenstatt is one of the oldest and largest of the modern ecclesial movements. Present on six continents, it is especially strong in South America, where the travels of the so-called Pilgrim Mother from home to home and popular pilgrimages to the Schoenstatt Shrines in Chile, Brazil, Argentina, Uruguay, Paraguay, Ecuador, and Mexico have proven a vital power for the New Evangelization and the strengthening of family life. Pope Francis is scheduled to meet with Schoenstatt leaders in Rome in October 2014 to mark the one hundredth anniversary of that Marian movement's foundation. That encounter with Schoenstatt will take place at the end of the Extraordinary Synod of Bishops to be held at the Vatican October 5–18 on the topic, "The Pastoral Challenges of the Family in the Context of the New Evangelization."

Present at the Holy Father's morning Mass at Domus Sanctae Marthae on May 18, 2013, were Kiko Argüello, Carmen Hernández, and Fr. Mario Pezzi, the initiators of the Neocatechumenal Way, which brought fifteen thousand members to St. Peter's Square later that same day. Argüello, a painter, presented to Pope Francis an icon of our Lady and several photographs of the "Great Mission" undertaken by the Neocatechumenal communities during the Year of Faith—a "Great Mission" that involved Christian witness through songs, testimony, and catechesis in more than ten thousand public squares in 120 countries during the five Sundays of Easter. Francis applauded this mission, telling the Neocatechumens, "Go into the public places and proclaim Jesus Christ, our Savior."[27] At a private audience with Neocatechumenal leaders in September 2013, Francis again thanked them for the "Great Mission," for the evangelical work undertaken

---

26. Chesnut, "Preferential Option for the Spirit," 6.
27. Arocho Esteves, "Neocatechumenal Way Initiators Meet with Pope Francis."

by the movement worldwide, especially in Asia, and for its fostering of vocations in extraordinary numbers to the priesthood.[28] Begun in 1964 in a slum in Madrid, where a young Kiko Argüello took up residence among the poorest, bringing with him only a Bible, a crucifix, and a guitar, the Neocatechumenal Way has become a major missionary force within the Church.

On Friday, September 13, 2013, Francis met in private audience with Maria Voce, president of the Focolare Movement founded during World War II by Chiara Lubich (1920–2008). Known worldwide for its effective ecumenical, interreligious, and youth work, the members of the Focolare—an Italian word meaning "hearth"—have a special charism for building unity and communion, drawing their inspiration from the prayer of Jesus, "that they may all be one" (John 17:21). The Focolare's dialogues with Protestant and Orthodox Christians, Jews, and Muslims are dear to the heart of Francis, as is their spirit of poverty. Their "economy of communion" projects (lauded by Pope Benedict XVI in his 2009 encyclical *Caritas in veritate*) have led to successful new models of business where a company's profits are shared with the workers and the poor. Answering to Voce's promise in May 2013 that the Focolare will "give testimony of a courageous and joyful Christianity," Pope Francis encouraged them "to keep going ahead with joy, because a Christian without joy will not attain anything."[29]

Later that same month, on September 30, 2013, Pope Francis met with participants in the International Meeting for Peace, organized by the Sant'Egidio Community. The only major modern ecclesial movement of international scope to have originated in Rome itself, Sant'Egidio was founded by Andrea Riccardi and other students in the late 1960s, during the time of the student revolt. At home in the Church as Vatican Council II had described it, Riccardi and his circle began meeting for prayer every evening and befriending the poor in the Roman shanties. Inspired by stories from the life of Saint Francis—his taming of the wolf of Gubbio, his meeting with the Sultan—the members of Sant'Egidio possess a charism of reconciliation that enabled them to broker the Mozambique Peace Agreement in 1994, ending sixteen years of civil strife. At the request of Pope John Paul II, Sant'Egidio has organized an annual interreligious day of prayer for peace in Assisi, starting in 1986. Every October 16, members of Sant'Egidio make a candlelight procession from Trastevere to the Jewish ghetto in Rome, to comemmorate and to atone for the arrest of the 1,022 Jews sent from Rome

---

28. "Pope Francis Receives Neocatechumenal Way Initiators."
29. See "Focolare President Promises Pope Testimony of Joy."

to Auschwitz. A living church "without walls," Sant'Egidio embodies the love for the poor, the striving for peace, and the missionary zeal—even at the cost of martyrdom—for which Pope Francis calls. "Evangelization is for us the mother of all works," writes Andrea Riccardi, "because it is the basis of the daily life, public and private, of each one of us ... Our people try to practice charity in their lives, especially for the little people and the poor."[30] Thanking Andrea Riccardi and the Sant'Egidio Community as a whole for their commitment to the work of peace and reconciliation, Pope Francis mingled praise with a heartfelt petition: "Keep the lamp of hope lit, [keep] praying and working for peace."[31]

It should be clear, from this brief survey of Pope Francis's encounters with the selected ecclesial movements, that there is a remarkable affinity between their thoughts, concerns, and actions and his. What one says, the other echoes. They speak, as it were, the same language. In his open letter of advice to the newly elected pope, for example, Jean Vanier, the founder of L'Arche—the ecclesial movement especially devoted to providing a home life for the mentally handicapped—encouraged Francis to "seek out the weak and the excluded." "My dream for the church," writes Vanier, "is that the people of God—that is to say, all of us—may find the way across the road to meet those in pain, those who feel excluded and are violated. But we cannot cross the road alone; we need to be in community."[32] This is also the dream of Francis, who writes in *Evangelii gaudium*, "I want a Church which is poor and for the poor. They have much to teach us ... We need to let ourselves be evangelized by them."[33]

Meeting in private audience with Pope Francis on October 11, 2013, Fr. Julián Carrón, the current leader of the international Commmunion and Liberation movement, reported to the Holy Father about the journey of CL since the passing in 2005 of its founder, Monsignor Luigi Giussani. Afterwards, Carrón reports, he was "amazed" to read "in the Pope's speech to the Plenary of the Pontifical Council for Promoting New Evangelization, some of the [very same] concerns that had emerged in our dialogue"—first, the need for "credible witnesses who make the Gospel visible with their lives, and also with their words, who reawaken the attraction for Jesus Christ, for the beauty of God"; second, the need to move "toward those

30. Riccardi, "St. Egidio Community," 169.
31. "Pope Francis' Address to the Participants International Meeting for Peace."
32. Vanier, "Seek Out the Weak," 18–19.
33. Pope Francis, *Evangelii gaudium*, 198.

who have lost faith and the profound meaning of life"; third, the need for "a common commitment to a pastoral project . . . that is well centered on the essential, that is, on Jesus Christ."[34]

The coincidence of topics, the echoing back and forth, is indeed significant. Francis—like John Paul II and Benedict XVI—clearly values the apostolic engagement of the movements and finds a divine beauty in their different charisms. In *Evangelii gaudium*, Francis speaks of *"charisms at the service of a communion which evangelizes."*[35] A Jesuit who has taken Saint Francis of Assisi as his special patron, Pope Francis is clearly identified with two movements of renewal in the Church's history.[36] In addition, though, Francis has been spiritually formed by the modern movements, with the result that he sees and addresses the Church as a whole as a movement— indeed, a movement of movements, a pilgrim people,[37] following the lead of Christ whose mission it was and is to "bring glad tidings to the poor . . . to proclaim liberty to captives and recovery of sight to the blind, to let the oppressed go free" (Luke 4:18).

Pope Francis and Communion and Liberation

In his conversation with Fr. Carrón, Francis shared that he had first encountered the Communion and Liberation movement in Buenos Aires in the early 1990s. It was, he said, a "breath of fresh air" for him—an encounter that led him to read the writings of Monsignor Giussani, founder of CL, and to learn from them.[38] Elsewhere, Bergoglio has written that Giussani's writings "have inspired me to reflect and have helped me to pray."[39]

---

34. Carrón, Letter to the Fraternity of CL. In this letter, Carrón wrote about his meeting with Pope Francis.

35. Pope Francis, *Evangelii gaudium*, 130–31.

36. Joseph Ratzinger points to five successive waves of renewal within the history of the Church as a manifestation of the "apostolic succession" that includes lay men and women, as well as clergy. He gives the Franciscan movement of the thirteenth century and the reform movement led by the Jesuits in the sixteenth century as examples, among many others. See Ratzinger, "Ecclesial Movements," 45–49.

37. Chapter 7 of *Lumen gentium* is titled "The Eschatological Nature of the Pilgrim Church and Her Union with the Heavenly Church." The fifth section of chapter 8 is titled "Mary, a Sign of Sure Hope and of Solace for God's People in Pilgrimage." See Abbott, *Documents of Vatican II*, 78 and 95.

38. Quoted in Carrón, Letter to the Fraternity of CL.

39. Bergoglio, "Gratitude of Buenos Aires," 14.

Indeed, prior to his election as pope, Bergoglio twice gave public talks in Buenos Aires at the International Book Fair to celebrate the publication of Spanish editions of Giussani's books. In 1999, Archbishop Bergoglio presented Giussani's classic text, *The Religious Sense* (*Il senso religioso*). In 2001, Cardinal Bergoglio commented upon Giussani's book *The Attraction That Is Jesus* (*L'attrattiva Gesù*). On both occasions, Bergoglio declared his personal gratitude to Giussani for "the good . . . that this man has done me, in my life as a priest, through the reading of his books and articles."[40] In an essay entitled "For Man," which appears in *A Generative Thought: An Introduction to the Works of Luigi Giussani*, Jorge Mario Bergoglio makes that same point about Giussani's books, saying, "They have taught me to be a better Christian."[41]

What Bergoglio singles out for special comment is Giussani's insight concerning the human being as a profoundly religious being, possessed with a "religious sense."[42] "Today the primary question we must face," he writes, "is not so much the problem of God—the existence, the knowledge of God—but the problem of the human, of human knowledge and finding in humans themselves the mark that God has made, so as to be able to meet with Him."[43] Because "we possess within us a yearning for the infinite," Bergoglio continues, "the human heart proves to be the sign of a Mystery, that is, of something or someone who is an infinite response,"[44] someone who alone can satisfy the heart's longing for love, for what is true and good and just and beautiful. The transformative encounter with God is thus, for Bergoglio, always an experience of the divine mercy that responds to our poverty and need. Embodied in Christ, the Word-Made-Flesh, divine mercy waits so eagerly for us that he comes to meet us while we are still on the way and draws us to himself. "Christian morality," Cardinal Bergoglio insists, "is the heartfelt response to a surprising, unforeseeable, 'unjust' mercy," a gratuity of grace.[45]

What is it in the life and writings of Luigi Giussani that Jorge Mario Bergoglio has found so attractive? What is it that he has learned from

---

40. See Premat, "Attraction of the Cardinal."
41. Bergoglio, "For Man," 79–83, quoted at 79.
42. See Giussani, *The Religious Sense*.
43. Bergoglio, "For Man," 79–80.
44. Ibid., 82.
45. See Premat, "The Attraction of the Cardinal," for this and other excerpts from the talk Bergoglio gave during the April 27, 2001, book presentation.

Giussani about the New Evangelization? I cannot answer that question with any completeness today, but I would like to mention three things that surely moved the Archbishop Bergoglio in the 1990s, when he first came in contact with CL and started reading Giussani. The first is the story of Giussani's conversion. According to Giussani's own testimony, he was a somewhat ordinary, "obedient and exemplary" young seminarian, "until one day something happened that radically changed [his] life" and ended its "banality."[46] As he describes it, the opening words of the Gospel according to John suddenly were illumined before the eyes of his soul. He read them and understood: "The Word of God [i.e., the response to the needs of the human heart, the ultimate object of everyone's desires for happiness] became flesh."[47] From this, Giussani derived "a certainty of presence—of Christ's presence in the world—in which there was hope to embrace everything" that happens as a sign of that presence, that event.[48] Giussani points here to what Pope Francis calls the thing "most essential" to Christianity, namely, the Christ event, the Incarnation, Jesus himself, God-with-us. Christ-centered, Communion and Liberation proposes (and here I quote Tony Hanna) "the presence of Christ as the only true response to the deepest needs of human life."[49]

The second is the story of Giussani's calling to begin what would become CL. Riding on a train one day, Giussani—then a professor at a seminary—overheard a conversation among three young men who were "terribly ignorant and full of prejudice about Christianity."[50] Moved by this encounter, Giussani resigned his position at the seminary and went to work as a teacher in a high school. He wanted to pass on the tradition of faith that he had learned from his mother and from his seminary teachers, but out of the conviction that "the presence of Jesus in the Church [is] the total response to the questions posed by the world," to the questions that arise from the human heart.[51] "The Christian's activity," Giussani affirms, "is by its very nature missionary, i.e., an urge to share the method of Christ, who created the Church to make him known throughout the world [and in every

---

46. Giussani, "Communion and Liberation," 155.
47. Ibid. The bracketed words appear in the printed text.
48. Ibid.
49. Hanna, *New Ecclesial Movements*, 34.
50. Giussani, "Communion and Liberation," 155.
51. Ibid., 156.

age]."⁵² Clearly Giussani's insight accords with that of Francis, who sees the Church as a missionary Church, an evangelizing Church, with good news for the world.

Ecclesial and christological, Giussani's insight is also profoundly anthropological. It emphasizes the restlessness of the human heart that seeks for a happiness only God can give. For Giussani, the Virgin Mary is the perfect example of someone whose human heart was completely open to God, who freely bore the impact of the encounter with the Infinite reality as no other purely human being ever has, and whose maternity extends to all Christians, indeed, to all whom Jesus died to save. As evidence of this "Mariological focus," Javier Prades López points to Giussani's comments on Dante's "Hymn to the Virgin" and to the short prayer Giussani recommended as a frequent daily ejaculation: "Veni Sancte Spiritus, veni per Mariam!" Come, Holy Spirit, come through Mary.⁵³

Pope Francis surely shares this "Mariological focus" and sets Mary before us as the great proclaimer of the Gospel of Joy. In *Evangelii gaudium*, Francis writes,

> With the Holy Spirit, Mary is always present in the midst of the people. She joined the disciples in praying for the coming of the Holy Spirit (Acts 1:14) and thus made possible the missionary outburst that took place at Pentecost. She is the Mother of the Church which evangelizes, and without her we could never truly understand the spirit of the new evangelization.⁵⁴

Pope Francis and the "Marian Style" in Evangelization

The last four long paragraphs of Pope Francis's Apostolic Exhortation, *Evangelii gaudium*, and the concluding prayer—a poem—emphasize the "Marian style" necessary for the New Evangelization. "There is a Marian 'style' to the Church's work of evangelization," Francis observes. "Whenever we look to Mary, we come to believe once again in the revolutionary nature of love and tenderness."⁵⁵ Pope Francis describes Mary herself as a charism, Jesus's gift to the Church from the cross ("Behold, your mother"

---

52. Ibid., 157.
53. Prades López, "Life of the Church," 61–102, especially 86–88.
54. Pope Francis, *Evangelii gaudium*, 284.
55. Ibid., 288.

[John 19:26]): "Jesus left us his mother to be our mother."[56] "Christ led us to Mary," writes the pope. "He brought us to her because he did not want us to journey without a mother, and our people read in this maternal image all the mysteries of the Gospel . . . The close connection between Mary, the Church and each member of the faithful, [is] based on the fact that each in his or her own way brings forth Christ,"[57] gives flesh to the Word. Contrary to those who have seen Mary as a hindrance to evangelization and ecumenism, Francis sees her person, her example, her spirit, and her intercession as key to the Church's success as a missionary Church.

Francis emphasizes Mary's openness to the promptings, gifts, and graces of the Holy Spirit—a quality foregrounded in all the new movements. Francis highlights the courage and the joy with which Mary hastened into the hill country to serve her cousin Elizabeth, carrying the Christ Child within her (Luke 1:39). In this and in her request for the miracle at Cana (John 2:1–11), she displays—as Francis notes—an attitude of tender caring and concern, of humble service, of closeness to life, that awakens in others a holy gratitude and praise. In Bethlehem's stable, Mary shared in the poverty of the poor and showed her Child as a sign of peace and salvation to the shepherds. Beneath the cross of her Son, she knew the piercing sorrow of a mother's love, the cost of sin, and the power of Christ's forgiveness. "This interplay of justice and tenderness, of contemplation and concern for others," writes Francis, "is what makes the ecclesial community look to Mary as a model of evangelization. We implore her maternal intercession that the Church may become a home for many peoples, a mother for all peoples, and that the way may be opened to the birth of a new world."[58]

Pope Francis venerates Mary especially as the "Untier (or Undoer) of Knots," the one who smooths out difficulties, as only a mother can.[59] The Marian style of evangelization proclaimed and exemplified by Pope Francis can be seen in the modern ecclesial movements and in the pope's own very evident, warm Marian devotion. The L'Arche movement, for example, makes regular pilgrimages to Lourdes and honors Mary as the merciful

56. Ibid., 285.
57. Ibid.
58. Ibid., 288.
59. "Undoer of Knots" is the title both of a Marian devotion and of a painting (c. 1700), which is venerated as a "Picture of Grace" at the Catholic Bavarian pilgrimage church of St. Peter am Perlach in Augsburg, Germany. Bergoglio saw this image during his studies in Germany and went on to promote devotion to our Lady under this title in South America.

mother.⁶⁰ The Neocatechumens love her as the very icon of a maternal, life-giving Church.⁶¹ The charismatics gather with her in prayer and praise.⁶² The Focolare, whose official name is the "Work of Mary," seeks to mirror Mary's love for Christ and humanity.⁶³ Communion and Liberation honors her as the one through whom the great Christ event, the Incarnation, takes place. Schoenstatt hails Mary as the "Great Missionary," the mother and model in Christ of the "new person in the new community."⁶⁴

The Schoenstatt Movement, founded in 1914 at the outbreak of World War I,⁶⁵ and the Fatima movement, founded in 1917, near the end of that same terrible war, are among the earliest and most explicitly Marian of the modern ecclesial movements. Fatima became a place of *de facto* pilgrimage in 1917 and exerted an immediate influence upon the political situation in Portugal,⁶⁶ but it effectively entered the world stage in the 1940s, with the disclosure of the so-called first and second secrets of Fatima and the founding of the international Blue Army. The spirituality of the Blue Army, officially approved as an ecclesial movement in 2010 by the Pontifical Council for the Laity under the title "World Apostolate of Fatima,"⁶⁷ is shaped by the specific requests and promises made by Our Lady of the Rosary at Fátima in 1917. Invoked as the Queen of Peace, Our Lady of Fátima (a place name with historical ties to Islam) has been and remains the special advocate for the cause of peace in the modern world.⁶⁸

---

60. See Spink, *Miracle*, 123–24 and 66–68.

61. See the icon of Mary painted by Kiko Argüello and featured in the header on the home page of the Neocatechumenal Way's website, http://www.camminoneocatecumenale.it/new/default.asp?lang=en.

62. See Alva, *Mary and the Catholic Charismatic Renewal Movement*.

63. The founder of the Focolare, Chiara Lubich, testifies that she discovered her vocation in 1939 during a pilgrimage to the Marian shrine in Loreto, Italy. Every Focolare conference center is called a Mariopolis (City of Mary).

64. See Kentenich, *Forming the New Person*.

65. See Niehaus, *New Vision and Life*.

66. See Bennett, *When the Sun Danced*.

67. See World Apostolate of Fatima, USA—Our Lady's Blue Army, home page (https://wafusa.org/). For additional Fatima-related associations recognized by the Church, see http://www.laici.va/content/laici/en/sezioni/associazioni/repertorio/world-apostolate-of-fatima.html.

68. Apostoli, *Fatima for Today*. Following the lead of Pope Benedict XVI, Apostoli argues that the mission of Our Lady of Fátima has not been completed with the end of World War II and the fall of the Iron Curtain but remains important and ongoing in the twenty-first century.

On May 13, 2013, Pope Francis dedicated his papacy to Our Lady of Fatima, who appeared to three Portuguese children in 1917 to call them—and through them, the people of the world—to repentance, fasting, and prayer, for the sake of peace. From his first homilies, Francis has called for peace and fasting, a turning away from the greed, the pride, and the worldly ambition that lead to violence. His is not an easy idea of peace. He knows the forces of violence and hatred at large in the world. In a stunning move in the midst of the international crisis precipitated by the use of chemical weapons in Syria, Pope Francis called for a worldwide day of fasting and prayer for peace on September 7, 2013—a prayer that effectively averted American airstrikes. As I write, another crisis—that in the Ukraine—renews the tensions between Russia and Europe that have led to bloody conflicts in the past.

In order to be an "instrument of peace" (Prayer of St. Francis) in the world, the Church as a whole, every Christian community, and each individual Christian must strive to be open to receive and ready to give Christ's peace (John 14:27). It must also, Francis warns, resist internal division and preserve unity in the midst of the challenging variety of gifts and charisms, the seeming confusion of voices, the greatness of the needs to be addressed, the creative tensions, and the competition of claims. "Diversity," writes Pope Francis, "must always be reconciled by the help of the Holy Spirit; he alone can raise up diversity, plurality and multiplicity while at the same time bringing about unity."[69]

Professing a fearless faith in the God of a peace that "surpasses all understanding" (Phil 4:7), in the Father of all, who "works everything to the good" (Rom 8:28), Pope Francis welcomes the diversity of the ecclesial movements alive in the Church and sees them as a manifestation of the Church's "Marian principle," ever open to the Holy Spirit, responsive to the concrete needs of the times, bringing Christ to others. Crowned with twelve stars, clothed with the sun (Rev 12), Mary is—for Francis—the "star of the New Evangelization" for a missionary church eager to proclaim "the joy of the Gospel . . . to the ends of the earth."[70]

---

69. Pope Francis, *Evangelii gaudium*, 131.
70. Ibid., 288.

7

The Hope of a Future for the Catholic Church

Maria Clara Lucchetti Bingemer

On February 11, 2013, still in the midst of Carnival, Benedict XVI stepped down as the bishop of Rome, the head of all churches. The seat of Peter became empty. Around the world perplexity entered the hearts and minds of people. As the reasons for such a courageous gesture by the pope, now emeritus, spread around the world in the days that followed, there were speculations and conjectures about who might become his successor and what it would mean in this very difficult moment for the Church.

The ecclesial community of the entire world turned their eyes towards Rome where such a unique situation was taking place. Awareness of the shadows that had swooped down on this institution, the oldest in the history of humankind, became clear. Painful and obscure facts that the media revealed spread extreme desolation among Catholics in every place and seeded insecurity in many of them. Questions appeared and fear joined expectation.

Once the conclave that chose the successor was over, the white smoke was celebrated not only by Catholics but by all those who know about the importance of Christianity in the history and culture of the West. In other words, men and women of goodwill, even though not members of this Church, felt orphaned by Benedict's resignation, which left behind all the pains and problems that were hurting the ecclesial institution. The white smoke announced that there was a new pope; the seat of Peter was not empty anymore.

In the heart of many, however, some questions and concerns remained. Was the new pope the appropriate choice to face the challenges that lay before him? What qualities are most desirable in the one whose mission is to lead the Church vigorously and vibrantly in the Third Millennium? Would the new pope be somebody capable of injecting enthusiasm in a whole faithful community in need of regaining hope?

As we approach the first anniversary of his pontificate, we can already see some directions Francis's ministry will follow and point to.

A Pope from the End of the World

The announcement of joy (*Gaudium magnum*) was made with shaking voice by the French cardinal. The name pronounced, Jorge Mario Bergoglio, astonished many and was questioned by others. Silence descended over St. Peter's Square as the crowd waited for the new pope to appear. Francis emerged on the Vatican balcony. Joyfully and with a warm voice he spoke a simple greeting: *Buona sera* (Good evening). Before blessing the people, the recently elected pope asked for a blessing from them. Besides that, he explained that his fellow cardinals had a tough time trying to give Rome a bishop. And they had to search for him at the end of the world. And so he presented himself as the bishop of Rome, Rome being the church that presides over all the other churches in charity. These first words had the power of the announcement of a new era for the Church, which could rejoice and breathe with hope.

From then on, the simplicity and humble style of the new pope enchanted everybody and took only some days to change the Church's image. His words are centered on a focus: the poor. And all of us Catholics who lived the conciliar spring discovered how much our ears were missing this word, repeatedly present on the lips of the pastor. Coming from the south of the planet, "the end of the world" where daily poverty and injustice damage the lives of human beings, Francis does not forget and does not allow anyone to forget at whose service the Church is, in charity. Faithful to the Gospel, he proclaims that the ones the world considers least are actually the most beloved by God, His preferred ones. Therefore, they should be the first and preferential option of Christ's Church.

The figure of the Argentine pope captures the world's attention. He radiates consistency and joy, which brings enthusiasm and becomes contagious to those who watch and listen to him. His first gestures reveal his profile little by little. For example, his asking the faithful assembled at St. Peter's Square to offer a prayer for him. Or the rejection of using official cars, the luxury of ermine cloaks, decorated miter, or gold woven ornaments. Or descending from the altar to kiss and caress a sick person during his inauguration ceremony. With his smile, always spontaneous, he charms everybody.

Francis's words reaffirm his gestures. No apocalyptic discourse tainted with anguish and perplexity. On the contrary, a positive attitude, a full desire to face the big challenges with trust and courage. Maybe this is the basic attitude that the Church needs to adopt. In a homily two days after his election, when he addressed his fellow cardinals in the Clementine Room at the Apostolic Palace in the Vatican, he pronounced words that sounded like a full program: "Let us never yield to pessimism, to that bitterness that the devil offers us every day."[1] This is an exhortation that is not a cheap consolation from an old man to others who likewise have reached the second half of life. Rather, it sounds like a recapturing of what constitutes the most profound and visceral content in Christian revelation. It is an invitation to live in the plain joy and peace of the Risen Christ even when everything looks contradictory to such a joyful mood.

A Name That Is a Full Program of Life and Work

The choice of name by a pope is not a question of taste or chance. A name reflects a project: the project of a new pontiff, pointing out to the world which theological lines, pastoral attitudes, and government policies will mark his pontificate.

The name Francis goes along this line. Immediately we can see the pope—who came from the South of the world where poverty and injustice prevail—manifest his desire to identify himself with the grand figure of Francis of Assisi, the *poverello* who loved poverty as his bride and served the poor as his most beloved brothers and sisters. It is the same Francis who heard from the Crucified, before whom he was praying in San Damian, the lovely request that sounds like a mandate: "Francis, rebuild my Church." At the very moment that Benedict XVI surprised the world by stepping down,

---

1. Pope Francis, "Audience with the College of Cardinals."

many shadows that obscured the face of the Church spread all over the world. The new pope has the mission to rebuild what became fragile and was almost destroyed. This was certainly one very good reason for adopting the name of Francis.

Nevertheless, besides being Argentine, *porteño*, Latin American, Pope Francis is also the first Jesuit pope in the entire history of the Church. Such a fact is rooted in the same Society of Jesus founded by Ignatius of Loyola at the beginning of modern times. Having lived through the calamitous situation in which the Church found herself, which among other things generated the Protestant Reformation, Ignatius was fully aware of how harmful to a true Christian life the honors and prestige of worldly living can be. Thus, in the constitutions of the new missionary order that he founded, Ignatius ordered explicitly that a Jesuit cannot accept ecclesial dignities. Such renunciation even became the object of a specific vow in the order, which all Jesuits must pronounce.

Across history, occasions arose in which this vow was waived due to an overriding ecclesial need, or an urgent circumstance, or an undeniable missionary priority. But the vow is the reason for having fewer Jesuit bishops or cardinals than from other orders. And there never was a Jesuit pope. It is proper to the spirit of the order not to seek or accept appointments to the hierarchy, unless God clearly shows His will in the opposite direction.

Jorge Mario Bergoglio was young when he entered the Society of Jesus, and in it he was formed and configured according to the unique style that the Spiritual Exercises of Saint Ignatius impress on any person who experiences them. What the media now treat as novel characteristics of the new pope—living in austerity, using public transportation instead of official cars, and strolling in the peripheries of the city to join the poor—are a reflex of the formation received in the school of the Pilgrim of Loyola, founder of the Society.

It can also be seen and verified that behind the new pontiff's chosen name appears the existence of another Francis besides the one from Assisi: Francis Xavier, noble Spaniard from Navarra, brilliant student at the University of Paris (Sorbonne), whose encounter with Ignatius changed his life. The closeness of his spiritual master and the experience of the Exercises polished his extraordinary temper and revealed the missionary that was sent to the East as a young man.

Thanks to this Francis, the Gospel arrived in India and Japan. At the age of forty-six, Xavier died at the doors of China. Very soon the fame of his sanctity became known around the world. And the Church made him patron of Catholic missions. Together with the *poverello* from Assisi, the missionary Xavier is present in the name of the new pope. This allows us to expect a pontificate marked by the saint of Assisi's love of the poor and the Jesuit from Navarra's passion and heroism.

Catholics who affirmed the conciliar springtime of the sixties and seventies, and who saw with great sadness the many steps forward turning into many steps backward in the eighties, feel a great hope for an ecclesial reform that Francisco has the mission to perform. To rescue the best of a Church that desires to embrace dialogue with the society and culture of the twenty-first century and the third millennium, Francis will have to touch on some absolutely crucial points. We have the feeling that this is already happening in the first year of his pontificate.

Returning to Vatican II

In some of the attitudes of Pope Francis, a return to Vatican II is clearly perceived as a priority and center of all ecclesial action. Sometimes these are subtle signals not perceived by everyone but certainly by those who experienced the breath of fresh air provoked by the conciliar springtime, and who subsequently suffered with the backward movement of the last thirty-five years. By action and words, Francis shows that Vatican II is back.

Ecumenism and Interreligious Dialogue

Already at the very beginning Francis has referred explicitly to Vatican II. Loyal to the ecumenical opening and its interreligious character, the pope—addressing on March 20 the delegates of other denominations and traditions—remembered John XXIII and his decision to call for a Council. He quoted explicitly from paragraph 4 of *Nostra aetate*, which assumes clearly the Jewish roots of Christianity in a positive and brotherly way.[2]

---

2. "The Church, therefore, cannot forget that she received the revelation of the Old Testament through the people with whom God in His inexpressible mercy concluded the Ancient Covenant. Nor can she forget that she draws sustenance from the root of that well-cultivated olive tree onto which have been grafted the wild shoots, the Gentiles. Indeed, the Church believes that by His cross Christ, Our Peace, reconciled Jews and Gentiles, making both one in Himself." Pope Paul VI, *Nostra aetate*, 4.

A week after his election, in a letter he sent to the chief rabbi of the Jewish community in Rome, he expressed a desire to "contribute to the progress of the relations among Jews and Catholics that they knew since Vatican II" and revealed himself as being one who wishes to be absolutely loyal to the spirit of openness and dialogue that was established with the conciliar event. Having been very present in the Jewish-Christian dialogue in his country of origin, home to one of the largest Jewish communities in the world, Francis stresses that he intends to continue this practice, not simply because he enjoys it but because it means continuing and following the guidelines of Vatican II, which proclaimed the existence of *semina Verbi* in religions other than Catholicism.

Ecclesial Collegiality

From the beginning of his papacy, even as he presented himself to the multitude congregated at St. Peter's Square, he demonstrated his faithfulness to conciliar ecclesiology. He has stressed repeatedly the definition of his ministry as "bishop of Rome," assuming all the ecumenical and institutional consequences such emphasis implies.

There in this very moment, those of us who lived through Vatican II and know its documents can recognize in the words of the pope collegiality as a distinctive mark of ministry and structure of the Church. Francis is very conscious of it and proclaims himself the bishop of the Church of Rome, which presides over the other churches in charity. With this he fills with hope the hearts of those who dream of a Church less centralized, more open and democratic—a Church more in accordance with the model of People of God, where charisms flourish and ministry can be exercised freely and fertilely.

In his own words,

> The church is the people of God ... Thinking with the church, therefore, is my way of being a part of this people. And all the faithful, considered as a whole, are infallible in matters of belief, and the people display this *infallibilitas in credendo*, this infallibility in believing, through a supernatural sense of the faith of all the people walking together ... When the dialogue among the people and the bishops and the pope goes down this road and is

genuine, then it is assisted by the Holy Spirit. So this thinking with the church does not concern theologians only.[3]

Liturgical Reform

In his celebrations, Pope Francis has indicated that the liturgical reform made by Vatican II came to stay. Those are simple celebrations, though full of reverent depth and meaning. Francis accepts and practices the path of the Council towards a simpler liturgy, closer to the people and more participative.

Certainly he must have practiced this way of celebrating in his beloved Argentina while visiting the *villas* on the outskirts of Buenos Aires, or the workers' neighborhoods and their homes. Or during his time as provincial of the Jesuits, accompanying celebrations in poor chapels distant from the more sophisticated churches.

It is encouraging to see the pope celebrating with simplicity, free of adornments and embellishments that not only disgust and alienate many people from liturgies but also scandalize many of them. It is a delicate point, because such liturgical reform has been rejected by ultraconservative groups.

Benedict XVI tried to handle these groups with extreme patience and delicacy. Francis appears to be more direct in his approach. By his celebrating according to the liturgical reform of Vatican II, he points out what he thinks should be done. For him, it is desirable that liturgy become a space of sharing and fraternity where everybody can celebrate as brothers the Supper of the Lord and live in fraternal and salvational communion.

In his own words,

> Vatican II was a re-reading of the Gospel in light of contemporary culture. Vatican II produced a renewal movement that simply comes from the same Gospel. Its fruits are enormous. Just recall the liturgy. The work of liturgical reform has been a service to the people as a re-reading of the Gospel from a concrete historical situation. Yes, there are hermeneutics of continuity and discontinuity, but one thing is clear: the dynamic of reading the Gospel, actualizing its message for today—which was typical of Vatican II—is absolutely irreversible.[4]

3. Spadaro, "A Big Heart Open to God."
4. Ibid.

Therefore, with Francis, Catholics can expect a return to Vatican II as the compass for a Church that recognizes the need for profound reform and transformation. Returning to the Council means coming back to the sources of the Gospel. And it promises to offer Catholics a Church more open to the world. In his own words, "The Church is called to come out of herself and to go to the peripheries, not only geographically, but also the existential peripheries: the mystery of sin, of pain, of injustice, of ignorance and indifference to religion, of intellectual currents, and of all misery."[5]

To those who expected an ideologue of anti-conciliar restoration, a very definitive answer was given. The ecumenical and interreligious theological and liturgical patrimony of Vatican II is fully part of the words and actions of the new pope. It allows us to expect that the winds of the Council will again refresh and shake a Church made stiff and wounded by the difficulties and challenges of the present moment.

The Return of the Poor as Content and as Method

Perhaps one of the more gratifying surprises that the new pontificate has brought with it is the return of the poor to the center of discourse and thought. In an audience with numerous journalists in the Paul VI Room, Pope Francis expressed his desires with the words of John XXIII: "How much would I like a poor Church for the poor." Those who have followed the first year of this pontificate knew that these were not mere words. Since the beginning, the themes of poverty, injustice, and the poor have been a distinctive mark of Francis's papacy.

The pontiff has revealed with great simplicity the exhortation that his good Brazilian friend and brother cardinal Claudio Humes, OFM, whispered in his ear as his election was confirmed: "Do not forget the poor." The name Francis is already part of this memory that cannot disappear, and which reorients the whole Church to the heart of the Gospel that inspires and moves him: the blessedness of the poor, chosen by God, announced by Jesus of Nazareth.

Francis's desire for a poor Church for the poor starts in his own person. His unpretentious and simple style, his worn-out shoes shown in the media all over the world, his insistence on giving away the luxury and privileges that correspond to him as head of state: all these put him in harmony with the prophetic inspirations of the conciliar period, like the magnificent

---

5. Bergoglio, "Evangelizing Implies Apostolic Zeal."

"Pact of the Catacombs" in which several bishops, many of them Latin Americans, decided to live a simple style of life, close to that of the poor.

Coming from "the end of the world," the latitudes where inequality and injustice prevail, Francis is very conscious that a large part of humankind lives in conditions of extreme and inhuman poverty. About that he has made emphatic declarations, most completely in the Aparecida document. These are his words: "We live, apparently, in the most unequal part of the world, which has grown the most yet reduced misery the least. The unjust distribution of goods persists, creating a situation of social sin that cries out to Heaven and limits the possibilities of a fuller life for so many of our brothers."[6] Not being even by far a radical revolutionary, Pope Francis, however, does not have a simplistic or assistentialist[7] view of the problem of poverty and the violence it inflicts on the Gospel and the lives of people, so many of whom do not have the essentials to live a dignified life. He often expresses his indignation about those conditions.

It is thus to be expected that during his pontificate, theology will be able to reflect again on the issues that were left behind due to a tense atmosphere existing among theologians and the magisterium of the Church. There are many issues that should be reclaimed: the whole question of the priority of the poor, of victims as the content of theological thinking; the whole perspective of the reflection that starts with the poor themselves and is directed and oriented by them; all the theological and pastoral efforts to transform a reality configured by structural injustice. Community and society—finally, humankind—long for such a reflection.

To those who had misgivings—and they were not few—about his election, due to negative comments made about his actions in Argentina

---

6. Allen, "CELAM Update." Bergoglio's words in the original Spanish are "estamos en la región aparentemente más desigual de mundo, la que más creció y menos redujo la miseria. Persiste la injusta distribución de los bienes, lo cual configura una situación de pecado social que clama al cielo y que excluye de las posibilidades de una vida más plena a muchos hermanos." Bergoglio, "Ponencia del Sr. Arzobispo en la V Conferencia del C.E.L.A.M."

7. For a definition of assistentialism, see Adriance, *Opting for the Poor*, 17–18 (endnote 4): "Assistentialism ... is a term commonly used in Brazil to denote what people in the United States would probably call the social casework approach to the problem of poverty. It usually consists of giving money, food, used clothing, and medical aid to people who are unable to work or whose employment does not provide adequate income to support their needs and/or the needs of their families. This concept has recently come under heavy attack by progressive Church people who point out the injustice of the whole income structure and who advocate replacing assistentialism with social activism aimed towards a more equitable distribution of ... wealth."—Ed.

during the somber and obscure period of military dictatorship, the pope seems to say that there is nothing to fear. Given the testimonies in his favor from persons like Adolfo Pérez Esquivel, Nobel Peace Prize winner, it can be verified, four decades after the fact, that the then-provincial of the Jesuits in Argentina, Jorge Bergoglio, helped those who needed shelter and protection during these terrible years in his country. When the La Plata River became a coffin to thousands of missing people in the so-called flights of death, the Jesuit Bergoglio obtained passports to allow people to cross borders and alerted persecuted people to hide when their names appeared on the lists of the dictatorship.

Some people continue to accuse him of not having done enough for such people, including the murdered Bishop Angelelli. However, those who did not live through the terrible tensions in these somber years should be more careful in making accusations. The circumstances were so dangerous and adverse that it was not easy to find the right balance. Many times the rule of the lesser evil had to prevail. Many times the silent and anonymous creation of conditions for avoiding the destruction of a life became the sole way to resist such a context of death.

All of us change and mature over time. Changing circumstances sometimes change attitudes. The same media that hurried to publicize suspicions about the Jesuit Bergoglio did not have the same urgency in revealing that, ten months before his election, in the Faculty of Theology of Buenos Aires, Archbishop Jorge Bergoglio reclaimed the memory of Fr. Rafael Tello, one of the pioneers of liberation theology in that country. Explaining his gesture, Bergoglio said, "These reparations that God does we must also do: the hierarchy, which at a certain moment judged it convenient to withdraw him from the faculty, today says that his thinking is valid. Even more, his work was foundational for evangelization in Argentina. I would like to thank God for that."[8]

In such words of the present pope pronounced quite recently, we find the wisdom of someone who reviews his attitudes and rejoices with the changes that happen in his conscience and that of the church he belongs to.

---

8. This is my own translation of the original Spanish (in Bergoglio, "Pobres en este mundo"): "Esas reparaciones que Dios hace: que la jerarquía que en su momento creyó conveniente separarlo hoy diga que su pensamiento es válido. Más aún, fue fundamento del trabajo evangelizador en Argentina. Quiero dar gracias a Dios por eso."

Conclusion: A New Fragrance for the Ecclesial Community

Pope Francis brought hope back to a discouraged Church. A new fragrance is being sensed in the air, and we taste the return of the Second Vatican Council. According to the Vaticanist Massimo Faggioli, "For Catholic theology, Vatican II is the *common ground* for diverse cultural and political sensitivities, common ground that resists sectarianism and revisionism: it is no coincidence that it is a non-European and non-North American pope who has inherited this task."[9]

Thanks to the pope who comes from the end of the world, the Church breathes with renewed hope and joy. It feels ready again to present to the world a new face for the third millennium.

Everything indicates that the Church of Francis will be one of openness and dialogue; ecumenical and sensitive to inter- and trans-religious differences, it will have no bias in regard to the different ways that people express their faith. It will celebrate devotedly and simply the mysteries of God, sheltering in its rituals those who believe but also those who search and desire to believe but have not came across faith. Or even those who do not search but feel incited by some points of the evangelical proposition.

Francis appears to be conscious that he cannot govern or decide alone. He is the bishop of Rome who presides over other churches in charity. Collegiality, so dear to the Council, appears to be back in his pontificate, building up a church model characterized by participation and collaboration among the different churches and the people living their faith.

It is to be expected also that a space is to be opened for those who desire and long to participate in a full way and not as second-class citizens: the laity, women and men, young people, the poor. His words about women and their importance in the Church, about gender and homosexuality and the search for God, and about those married in a second union, are there already calling attention and giving hope to many Catholics who felt rejected and looked on with suspicion by their Church. Also encouraging was his presence in Rio de Janeiro on World Youth Day, where more than three million people, mostly youngsters, filled Copacabana beach in the cold and

---

9. Faggioli, "Francesco, ritorno al Concilio Vaticano II." The article was translated from Italian into Portuguese by Moisés Sbardelotto and published online at http://www.ihu.unisinos.br/noticias/518643-francisco-retorno-ao-concilio-vaticano-ii-artigo-de-massimo-faggioli. The English translation was later published in Faggioli's 2015 book *Pope Francis: Tradition in Transition*, published by Paulist Press.

rain to listen to his words of hope and joy. All of these people and more look towards the church of Rome with hope. They are the ones that could help the pope guide the flock that has been entrusted to him, hurt and diminished, in the direction of a new spring compatible with the challenges that the current momentum presents.

To finish with his own words:

> The church sometimes has locked itself up in small things, in small-minded rules. The most important thing is the first proclamation: Jesus Christ has saved you. And the ministers of the church must be ministers of mercy above all. . . .
>
> . . . The proclamation of the saving love of God comes before moral and religious imperatives. Today sometimes it seems that the opposite order is prevailing.[10]

> I see clearly that the thing the church needs most today is the ability to heal wounds and to warm the hearts of the faithful; it needs nearness, proximity. I see the church as a field hospital after battle. It is useless to ask a seriously injured person if he has high cholesterol and about the level of his blood sugars! You have to heal his wounds. Then we can talk about everything else. Heal the wounds, heal the wounds. . . . And you have to start from the ground up.[11]

---

10. Spadaro, "A Big Heart Open to God."
11. Ibid.

8

A Journalist's Notes on Pope Francis and His Testimony

The Call to the Worldwide Church for "Pastoral Conversion"

ANDREA TORNIELLI

There is something unmistakable that everyone has realized since the evening of March 13, 2013, when the conclave elected a pope coming from "the end of the earth." The gestures, the words, the testimony of Francis have touched and continue to move many people throughout the world.

It is worth remembering for a moment the evening of the election, when the new pope, appearing from the central window of Saint Peter's, asked the whole square to pray the Our Father, Hail Mary, and Glory Be. Before giving his blessing to the men and women of his new dioceses and of the whole world, the pope asked the crowd—God's people—to pray for him.

The election was incredibly speedy, as it was for his predecessor, and this was a surprise. Another surprise was the historical announcement of Pope Benedict XVI's abdication, which had taken place the previous month. Pope Benedict was indeed the first pope in two thousand years of Church history who abdicated because of old age.

In my opinion, there are two elements that stand out and can help explain the attention and fondness aroused by Pope Francis, even in ideologically distant groups. This attention and fondness does not appear to be diminishing, despite the predictions of an end of the "honeymoon" with the media, which were advanced by those who sometimes seem to miss the recent times, when the Church was "under attack."[1]

The first of these two elements is his personal testimony of the message of the Gospels, namely, big and small gestures, as well as the small or big daily choices that he makes; and his ability to meet and speak to everyone, by simply being himself. All of this has made him not only believable but, above all, approachable. The pope is now perceived by many people all over the world as being one of them.

We need only think of the embrace with the sick, the suffering, and the children. We need only think of the time he spends among people before and after Wednesday's general audiences: the pope passes almost one and a half hours each Wednesday greeting people. And we are all familiar with the images of the hundreds of sick people who were received in the Vatican last November. Francis spent more than two hours greeting them, one by one. Some might say, "Does the pope have nothing better to do?" I think the answer to that is that, for the pope, there *is* nothing better to do!

The pope also shows this through the visitation of all the Roman parishes, namely, his diocese. Instead of relegating the visits to Sunday mornings, when the pope has limited time due to the twelve o'clock Angelus, forcing him to leave the parish in a hurry after celebrating Mass, Francis solves the problem by paying the visit on a Sunday afternoon, so he can take the time he needs. It so happened, therefore, that Francis spent over three hours in a parish, meeting every last one of the people there, including a delegation of people demonstrating for a council house [public housing].

The shepherd must have "the smell of the sheep":[2] he must be in front of the people, to guide them; among the people, to know them and share with them hopes and fears; and behind the people, to prevent some from losing their way. It is the image, or better yet the testimony, of a Church that is really close to the people and lays its cheek on the cheek of those who suffer and live in pain, and those who are in material, physical, or spiritual difficulties.

It is the testimony of a Church that is not afraid of tenderness, the silent tenderness that has as its role model St. Joseph. "We must not be afraid of tenderness!" Francis has repeated this phrase since the very beginning of his new appointment as bishop of Rome. And he reiterated this in my

---

1. Rodari and Tornielli, *Attacco a Ratzinger*.
2. Pope Francis, "Homily for the Chrism Mass."

interview with him, which I published in *La Stampa* and *Vatican Insider* on December 15, 2013:

> When Christians forget about hope and tenderness they become a cold Church, that loses its sense of direction and is held back by ideologies and worldly attitudes, whereas God's simplicity tells you: go forward, I am a Father who caresses you. I become fearful when Christians lose hope and the ability to embrace and extend a loving caress to others. Maybe this is why, looking towards the future, I often speak about children and the elderly, about the most defenseless that is. Throughout my life as a priest, going to the parish, I have always sought to transmit this tenderness, particularly to children and the elderly. It does me good and it makes me think of the tenderness God has towards us.[3]

The second element that explains the pope's attractiveness is his teachings, which take place during the homilies of the Mass celebrated daily in the Casa Santa Marta. They are short comments on the readings of the day, delivered every morning—a short and simple style of preaching, reminiscent of Albino Luciani (Pope John Paul I)—which are at the same time deep and able to reach people's hearts. These teachings accompany many believers each and every day, more than big encyclicals or intellectual cultural debates could ever hope to do.

The message that Francis considers most important, as he himself proclaimed in his homily at the Vatican parish of St. Anna on March 17, 2013, is that of divine mercy. The pope told the Brazilian bishops during his trip to Rio de Janeiro in July 2013,

> Concerning pastoral conversion, I would like to recall that "pastoral care" is nothing other than the exercise of the Church's motherhood. She gives birth, suckles, gives growth, corrects, nourishes, and leads by the hand . . . So we need a Church capable of rediscovering the maternal womb of mercy. Without mercy we have little chance nowadays of becoming part of a world of "wounded" persons in need of understanding, forgiveness, love.
>
> We need a Church capable of walking at people's side, of doing more than simply listening to them; a Church which accompanies them on their journey; a Church able to make sense of the "night" contained in the flight of so many of our brothers and sisters.[4]

---

3. Tornielli, "Never Be Afraid of Tenderness."
4. Pope Francis, "Meeting with the Bishops of Brazil."

Francis also said in the course of his interview with the editor-in-chief of *La Civiltà Cattolica*,

> I dream of a church that is a mother and shepherdess. The church's ministers must be merciful, take responsibility for the people and accompany them like the Good Samaritan, who washes, cleans and raises up his neighbor. This is pure Gospel. God is greater than sin. The structural and organizational reforms are secondary—that is, they come afterward. The first reform must be the attitude. The ministers of the Gospel must be people who can warm the hearts of the people, who walk through the dark night with them, who know how to dialogue and to descend themselves into their people's night, into the darkness, but without getting lost. The people of God want pastors, not clergy acting like bureaucrats or government officials. The bishops, particularly, must be able to support the movements of God among their people with patience, so that no one is left behind. But they must also be able to accompany the flock that has a flair for finding new paths.
>
> Instead of being just a church that welcomes and receives by keeping the doors open, let us try also to be a church that finds new roads, that is able to step outside itself and go to those who do not attend Mass, to those who have quit or are indifferent. The ones who quit sometimes do it for reasons that, if properly understood and assessed, can lead to a return. But that takes audacity and courage.[5]

Something obvious to anyone who attempts to observe reality—and is not influenced by nostalgic prejudices, tastes in ecclesiastical clothing, or even by the self-referential debate of some intellectual circles who have often reduced the deep teachings of Pope Benedict to the model of a "law and order" church—is that these first eleven months have been a breath of fresh air for many.

It is exactly in Francis's attitude of "humility and closeness" and his going back to the essentials of Christian faith and the radicalism of the Gospel that we can find the distinctive trait of this first year. A closeness that can "warm hearts" and was manifested in all its force during the first papal trip outside of Rome, in July 2013, when Francis went to the Italian island of Lampedusa to visit the migrants who arrive on old, unsafe boats, which too often become coffins drowned in the abyss. This closeness also emerged during the trip to Brazil, culminating in a visit to a Rio de Janeiro favela.

---

5. Spadaro, "A Big Heart Open to God."

During the Vigil of Pentecost, in May 2013, Francis said,

> If we step outside ourselves we find poverty. Today—it sickens the heart to say so—the discovery of a tramp who has died of the cold is not news . . . Today, the thought that a great many children do not have food to eat is not news. This is serious, this is serious! We cannot put up with this! Yet that is how things are. We cannot become starched Christians, those over-educated Christians who speak of theological matters as they calmly sip their tea. No! We must become courageous Christians and go in search of the people who are the very flesh of Christ, those who are the flesh of Christ![6]

On November 29, 2013, in a dialogue with the superiors of religious orders, Francis said,

> It is not a good strategy to be at the center of a sphere. To understand we ought to move around, to see reality from various viewpoints. We ought to get used to thinking. I often refer to a letter of Fr. Pedro Arrupe, who had been General of the Society of Jesus. It was a letter directed to the Centros de Investigación y Acción Social (CIAS). In this letter, Fr. Arrupe spoke of poverty and said that some time of real contact with the poor is necessary. This is really very important to me: the need to become acquainted with reality by experience, to spend time walking on the periphery in order really to become acquainted with the reality and life experiences of people. If this does not happen, we then run the risk of being abstract ideologists or fundamentalists, which is not healthy.[7]

The "pastoral conversion" the pope asks of the whole Church has therefore much to do with moving outside of ourselves and outside of the self-referential internal debates that the world does not understand, in order to reach what Francis calls the "existential and geographical periphery," meaning both the actual, physical suburbs and the mental periphery of desperation and lack of meaning, which can be found among the most expensive homes of the city.

From this point of view, I think it is wrong to claim that Pope Bergoglio speaks and acts in this way because he comes "from the end of the world," from Argentina. Better yet, this is true if we truly know what a capital city like Buenos Aires is really like. The pope comes from "the end of the earth" but at the same time he comes from the heart of the modern

---

6. Pope Francis, "Address on the Vigil of Pentecost."
7. Spadaro, "Wake Up the World."

world, with its challenges and contradictions. It is true that Bergoglio did not travel much, because as a bishop, whenever he was on a trip, he wished to go back *da mi esposa*, to his bride, meaning his diocese (and for this reason he even criticized the attitude of those "airport bishops" who are always traveling). He did not travel much but he had the world in his home: the relationships to other Christian denominations, to other religions, the challenge of secularization, the results of a certain kind of capitalism, the inequalities, the poverty...

And as far as poverty is concerned, it is striking to see how the Church teaching on social doctrine, proclaimed by the popes of the twentieth century, has become in today's world dangerously leftist, so much so that it is wrongly labeled as "Marxist" by those unfamiliar with both Marxism and the social doctrine of the Church.

The apostolic exhortation *Evangelii gaudium*, the real programmatic document of the pontificate, says, "An evangelizing community gets involved by word and deed in people's daily lives; it bridges distances; it is willing to abase itself if necessary, and it embraces human life, touching the suffering flesh of Christ in others." An evangelizing community "stand[s] by people at every step of the way, no matter how difficult or lengthy this may prove to be. It is familiar with patient expectation and apostolic endurance... It cares for the grain and does not grow impatient at the weeds."[8]

The main criterion for renewal is not any specific theological thought or ecclesiastical line of thinking but "a missionary impulse capable of transforming everything, so that the Church's customs, ways of doing things, times and schedules, language and structures can be suitably channeled for the evangelization of today's world rather than for her self-preservation."[9]

Pope Francis believes changes need to be made to the way in which the Gospel is announced—for example, the way in which certain issues that are part of the Church's moral teaching are represented in the media is called into question. The "occasionally biased media coverage" of the Church's teaching means its message "runs a greater risk of being distorted or reduced to some of its secondary aspects." This happens when "certain issues which are part of the Church's moral teaching are taken out of the context which gives them their meaning."[10]

---

8. Pope Francis, *Evangelii gaudium*, 24.
9. Ibid., 27.
10. Ibid., 34.

According to Francis, moral action must be the fruit of a life enlightened by the gospel.

> Pastoral ministry in a missionary style is not obsessed with the disjointed transmission of a multitude of doctrines to be insistently imposed. When we adopt a pastoral goal and a missionary style which would actually reach everyone without exception or exclusion, the message has to concentrate on the essentials, on what is most beautiful, most grand, most appealing and at the same time, most necessary.[11]

The pope quoted St. Thomas to stress that "as far as external works are concerned, mercy is the greatest of all the virtues"[12] for a human intelligence illuminated by faith. The mission of announcing the joy of the Gospel takes into account human limitations and the condition in which humans live, marked by original sin and the external influences we are subject to.

I believe that in order to fully comprehend the "pastoral conversion" that Pope Francis asks of the whole Church, it is necessary to reread the pages of the Gospel, those pages that should be the constant point of reference in the life of every Christian. If we look at the dynamics of the Gospel tales, we realize that Jesus attracted the sinners; he did not push them away or repel them. He gave testimony of a boundless love and always embraced before he judged: let us think of the consolation of the adulterous woman, who, instead of being damned, is forgiven. The heart of the Christian message is the embrace of a God who loves us for who we are and always welcomes and forgives us. It is in that embrace that we recognize ourselves: small, sinful, and in need of mercy.

In this sense, the testimony and the words of the pope are as traditional—in the true Christian tradition—as they can be. And if his words—his insistence upon divine mercy—also bother some people within the Church, we should ask how and why Christianity has lost this fundamental and attractive connotation.

In response to what is happening, various attitudes are possible. There are those in the Church who claim to already be doing what the pope wishes, and there are those who feel entrenched in their own schemes, who try to reduce his testimony and teachings to their own thoughts on the Church. There are those who criticize and obstruct in the name of an alleged tradition: it is the problem of those who collect vestments and crystallize the

---

11. Ibid., 35.
12. Ibid., 37.

liturgy and the Church's message with timeless nostalgia for the *ancien regime* of the past. There are those who pick and choose among the pope's speeches in order to feel justified. And there are those who are waiting for this pontificate to end, too.

But the "pastoral conversion" that Francis asked of the whole Church will only be realized if the bishops, the priests, and every ecclesiastical entity, as well as every faithful man and woman, will allow the pope's example and words to question themselves personally. Everyone, none excluded.

> We need to invoke the Spirit constantly. He can heal whatever causes us to flag in the missionary endeavor. It is true that this trust in the unseen can cause us to feel disoriented: it is like being plunged into the deep and not knowing what we will find. I myself have frequently experienced this. Yet there is no greater freedom than that of allowing oneself to be guided by the Holy Spirit, renouncing the attempt to plan and control everything to the last detail, and instead letting him enlighten, guide and direct us, leading us wherever he wills.[13]

I would like to conclude with this quotation by the pope, who explains very well what it means to evangelize:

> In fact, when, in the view of many people, the Catholic faith is no longer the common patrimony of society and, often, seen as seed threatened and obscured by the "gods" and masters of this world, only with great difficulty can the faith touch the hearts of people by means [of] simple speeches or moral appeals, and even less by a general appeal to Christian values . . . Simply proclaiming the message does not penetrate to the depths of people's hearts; it does not touch their freedom; it does not change their lives. What attracts is, above all, the encounter with believing persons who, through their faith, draw others to the grace of Christ by bearing witness to him.[14]

The pope who said this was not Francis but Benedict XVI, that Benedict who was often forgotten and pushed into the conservative "Ratzingerian" cliché (I personally believe that Ratzinger was not "Ratzingerian"). It was May 2010, and Benedict XVI was addressing the bishops of Portugal. These words help us understand how Bergoglio's and Ratzinger's outlooks on the Church and the world are in tune, even with the different inflections

---

13. Ibid., 280.
14. Pope Benedict XVI, "Meeting with the Bishops of Portugal."

and different personalities, character, and training. But this is and always will be the richness of the Church: if there had been absolute continuity throughout all of time, the pope would now be a fisherman in Galilee . . .

9

Francis: Renovator, Reformer, or Revolutionary? Two Reflections

SERGIO RUBIN AND FRANCESCA AMBROGETTI

Sergio Rubin

It gives me great honor to participate in this conference where important religious figures and learned academics have offered an enlightening analysis of Pope Francis's pontificate. As a journalist for more than thirty years, I focus on religious issues for the secular media of Argentina, and it's that perspective from which I'm speaking here. First and foremost, I have to confess that, unlike the 2005 conclave when I considered Jorge Bergoglio to be *papabile*, in 2013, I didn't—apart from, a few days before his election, writing in the newspaper and stating on television that, based on Vatican sources, he was again a candidate. I thought his time had passed. However, I thought that the Church—battered by an enormous number of problems—must have the courage in this moment to surprise with a pontiff who could wrest it from the eye of the storm and revitalize its religious life. So, the announcement of his election as Peter's successor evoked in me, above all, great surprise, then overwhelming joy and, ultimately, immense fear because of the tremendous challenges awaiting him.

The goal of this talk is not to spend our time in an analysis of how Jorge Bergoglio came to be Pope Francis. But I do want to emphasize the boldness of the cardinals in taking a chance this time on something new: the first pope from the New World; the first pope from the periphery—from "the end of the world," he would say; the first Jesuit pope. And I also want to emphasize the fact that this something new involved a change in profile (more pastoral) and in approach (more open) along with the strong social concern of the man now in Peter's chair. In that sense, I find certain similarities with the succession of Pius XII and the happy arrival of John XXIII. It confirmed for me the Church's capacity to "reinvent" itself, above and beyond the action of the Holy Spirit in the eyes of faith. Now, that said, those characteristics of Jorge Bergoglio were already familiar to those of us following the thought and actions of the then-archbishop of Buenos Aires. And they were particularly familiar to me and my dear colleague and friend Francesca Ambrogetti because of the book *El jesuita*. Published in 2010, this book was based on two years of conversations we had with Cardinal Bergoglio.

Based on the priest and bishop Jorge Bergoglio's track record and an analysis of his nearly complete first year as a pontiff whose words and gestures sparked so much enthusiasm, it's fitting to ask if we are witness to a renovator, reformer, or revolutionary. Again, my approach to these questions is that of a journalist who reports on religious issues and who bridges the gap between the media and a diverse public—a journalist who must be properly trained but who must communicate as clearly and directly as possible. When reporting on religious topics, the challenge is greater because religion invokes a transcendental dimension, which necessarily tends to subject us to charges of "reductionism" or purely political interpretations. Moreover, from a media perspective, what matters is not only what a Church or institutional exponent wants to convey in words and actions but also what the audience processes and decodes from that. That's why it's not only important who Francis really is but also how we present him and how he is perceived.

Is he a renovator? Yes, if by "renovation" we mean having renewed enthusiasm among the faithful; of this there is no doubt. In many parts of the world, there is talk of not a few Catholics returning to the faith, even to church itself, to Mass. Here in the United States, I have heard stirring testimony from people (not limited to Italians or my fellow Argentinians) who have moved beyond disillusionment. Francis's witness to austerity and proximity to all people (especially the very poor), his understanding words (perhaps most celebrated is the question put to reporters on the return flight to Rome after his visit to Brazil: who am I to judge a gay person?)—all of these gestures had an impact that makes any commentary unnecessary. And these gestures have had a greater educational impact than any encyclical. In the same way, Francis's desire for more transparency in the Church and more simplicity among the clergy was met with great welcome. In a world full of words and a Church prolific in documents that very few read, his witness in a media society made him a great communicator. Even with his splendid smile, he conveyed with unique power the joy of the Gospel. As *Time* magazine said, "He has not changed the words"—because he hasn't changed any church teachings—"but he's changed the music."[1] I like this metaphor. And I have no doubt that he is a renovator.

Is Francis a reformer? As I previously noted, there are no changes to Church teachings. But it seems to me there are some signs that there will be changes during his pontificate, or at least that discussion will begin. The best example at hand is the issue of the ban on divorced and remarried Catholics receiving communion. It's true that Benedict XVI never closed the door on reviewing this highly controversial point, but Francis seems ready to tackle it. The upcoming Synod on the Family will be a great test. What is more, the extensive questionnaire on family difficulties that he sent to the bishops around the world suggests that we are on the eve of a broader and more realistic discussion of these issues in the Church. There are many issues that point to a series of changes underway: the changes being planned in the Roman Curia, the end of "careerism" among the clergy and the curbing of honorific titles, the deeper collegiality being sought, the new administrative structures being considered, the future appointment of women to key institutional positions, etc. How far Francis will go—or, perhaps better said, how far he'll be able to go—is a question that time will answer. I have no doubts that he wants to make changes, but in a prudent and measured way. His most pressing need is to give new life to the Gospel message. In short, Francis is also a reformer.

Is he a revolutionary? I must admit that this question is almost an accusation. However, I think that he *is* a revolutionary in the sense that he's carrying out a kind of cultural revolution in the Church. Because, in my opinion, after centuries during which the institution seemed to favor guilt and condemnation (or, at least, that's how a good part of society perceived it), Francis is returning love to its place front and center. It's not that he wants to abolish sin, as has been erroneously stated, but rather to recall that

---

1. Gibbs, "Pope Francis, the Choice."

the redemptive power of love is stronger than all human weakness. And placing love first means not only being understanding and knowing how to forgive but also witnessing that to others. It means not obsessing over sexual issues, talking not only about protecting the beginning of life but also its entire process until natural death. It means committing ourselves seriously to social justice and peace. It means dialogue and putting ourselves in someone else's shoes. It means respecting the freedom of all but not silencing the Christian message. It means proclaiming the Gospel with joy, being happy that we are here and knowing also that there is eternal life. In the final analysis, the Christian message is lovingly and peacefully revolutionary.

It's at this point that we need to ask if Catholics—the clergy and the faithful—will also be renovators, reformers, and revolutionaries like Francis. Will they merely applaud him, or will they actually follow him?

The new pope's first inspiration was to have taken the name of the great saint of the poor. There's an entire agenda there—let's not forget that St. Francis of Assisi was a renovator, a reformer, and a revolutionary.

Francesca Ambrogetti

I would like to begin with a personal story about the beginnings of the book *El jesuita* (the title in English is *Pope Francis: Conversations with Jorge Bergoglio*), which I published with Sergio Rubin in 2010. It was an *ante litteram* biography, intended as the memoirs and epilogue of a valued but largely unknown South American cardinal, and it ended up becoming the prologue of a great pope.

In early April 2001, I called the Office of the Archdiocese of Buenos Aires to invite Cardinal Bergoglio to a meeting with foreign correspondents. To my utter amazement, he himself took the call; there was no secretary for me to pass through. That was the first of many powerful surprises I experienced—surprises that went global on March 13, 2013, and that persist today and seem destined to continue. The second surprise was that he accepted my invitation (he was not inclined to talk to the press), and the third was his refusal to be picked up, saying that he would travel, as he always did, by public transit. Let's just say that in Buenos Aires, this isn't usually the most comfortable way to get from one place to another.

On the day of the meeting, April 10, he arrived alone and on foot, as the bus stop was some two hundred meters away. He was dressed as a simple priest and carrying his briefcase, the very one he still uses. We were waiting for him at the door with some colleagues, and one of them asked me if I was sure he was the cardinal or if he might have sent one of his assistants. And more surprise and astonishment were in store: his simple, approachable, friendly, and warm demeanor was such a contrast to the knowledge, intelligence, and clear perception of reality with which he answered our questions. He talked about the Argentine crisis that would come to a head at the end of that year, about the global state of affairs, about the situation of the Church and his own vision for it. It became clear to me in that moment that Bergoglio had a way of thinking and living a coherent life that deserved to be made known through a book. We asked him what he thought the profile of the future pope should be, and he answered very emphatically and without hesitation: *a shepherd*. We were all very far from imagining, as was he, that almost exactly twelve years later he would be the one named by the College of Cardinals to lead a church immersed in a profound and almost unprecedented crisis—to guide it toward what many consider a crucial renewal and structural reform on many levels (in his contribution to this volume, Sergio Rubin addresses these two challenges in greater depth, based on his experience as a well-known journalist specializing in religious affairs). As for the word *revolution*, feared by many and deeply desired by others, I would dare to say that Francis is trying to bring it about in the most difficult of all places: in our conscience. And this is fully consistent with the Christian message. I believe that change is possible only if it is born in the heart as well as the mind, in our ways of thinking and feeling, as Francis continuously challenges us. It is no coincidence that one of his favorite phrases is this: "Open your mind to your heart."

People from many different perspectives have offered many definitions for what the pope is doing; they are all valuable and reflect different facets of the changes he is creating. But there is one that seems to me the most moving, and it belongs to Juan Carlos Scannone. An Argentine Jesuit and philosophy professor who taught Bergoglio in the seminary, Scannone says that Francis is leading "the revolution of tenderness."[2] The tenderness and compassion he feels and shows toward all those who suffer spark in others a response, a reaction. According to Scannone, it is what philosophers and linguists call the pragmatic moment. In what Bergoglio says and how he says it, in his nonverbal communication and the enthusiasm of

2. Ambrogetti, "Pope Leads 'Revolution of Tenderness.'"

the response he receives, Scannone believes we can find great hope for the Church and humanity.

Defined by some as the "first global pope," Francis is daily broadening the horizon of his message, and it stands to reason that such a transformative, reformist, and revolutionary pontiff would undoubtedly create resistance. Strangely, though, he is encountering this resistance within his very own Church, while, with just a few exceptions, being met with growing consensus among those outside of it.

I have wondered what kind of Church and world the overwhelming majority of cardinals had in mind when they voted for Jorge Bergoglio as Peter's successor. I can recall the far-sightedness of other conclaves, and I think especially of the one in 1963 that elected Paul VI. This was the pope who invited Soviet leaders to the Vatican. He encouraged a thaw between two great blocs whose hostility toward each other could have led to a destructive, large-scale armed conflict. And then there's the 1978 conclave that chose the Polish pontiff, John Paul II, as the appropriate leader in a world where the fall of the Berlin Wall would mark the beginning of new and different global power balances.

I think the cardinals who elected Bergoglio must have had in mind the great challenges of today's world. And I would identify the following as some of those challenges:

1. *The growing concentration of wealth that marginalizes vast social sectors and occurs at different levels in almost all countries, condemning many nations throughout entire regions of the world to poverty*

The recent economic crises have created pockets of poverty in wealthy countries that are discovering the periphery within their own borders, while emerging nations are seeking a more prominent role that has so far been denied them. And who better to advocate for a more just world than the Argentine cardinal who came from so far away?

Who better than the one from "the end of the world," the first pope from a megalopolis, one of those massive urban conglomerates where all the contrasts, all the good and the bad of our society come together?

Who better than the one who worked in silence and, with his own hands, touched the outer limits of poverty in the outlying slums of Buenos Aires? The one who trudged through the mud many times on rainy days for the religious processions in the *villas miserias*. In these shantytowns where streets are unpaved, he would come away with his black pants—the same ones he wears today—dirty and wet all the way up to the knees.

Who better than the one who defined injustice as *intolerable* in a favela of Rio de Janeiro, an emblem of marginalization and extreme poverty?

Who better than the one who, in a meeting with the United Nations' Executive Council, urged the members to challenge all forms of injustice, oppose the economy of exclusion, and work together to promote a truly global ethics movement?

And in this context is the tragedy of the displaced, those who are seeking a better life but doing so under desperate and difficult circumstances that often take that very life away. And the tragedy of these migrants often creates serious problems for the countries and communities they hope and attempt to reach.

And who better to understand this kind of uprooting, this rootlessness, than Jorge Bergoglio, whose family relocated from Italy to Argentina at the turn of the last century? This rootlessness was something he encountered again in his pastoral work in the slums of Buenos Aires, where there's a high population of immigrants from other Latin American countries. He showed his deep understanding of this experience when he decided that his first trip outside of Rome would be to Lampedusa. An image of hope for thousands of people trying to flee Africa, this island lies in a beautiful sea that became, for many of them, a watery grave.

Francis's trip to Lampedusa will surely not be his last journey to other borders between rich and poor countries where similar tragedies take place.

2. *The many peace-threatening hot spots around the world, especially in the Middle East*

And who better to work for peace—a peace whose knot is tightest in the Middle East—than the Argentine cardinal with a longtime commitment to ecumenism and interreligious dialogue?

Who better than the cardinal who fostered, like no other, rapprochement with Judaism but also with Muslims and representatives of other faiths? The one who listens to all and believes in, and encourages, the culture of encounter. The one who wanted to travel to the Holy Land so that he could speak out firmly and determinedly from there. The one who managed to bring together in prayer the presidents of Israel and Palestine, an unprecedented meeting that few believed possible and that charted a path for peace. This peace must continue to be a goal on the international horizon despite the new and recent escalation of violence. Francis preached against this violence and will continue, as always, to do so: with words, with examples, with actions—with the way he lives each moment of his life.

3. *Care for the planet, our human "home," which is today in danger*

And who better to warn us of this danger than the pope, who comes from a continent that still has many natural resources? Who better than the pope who chose the name Francis in honor of the saint of the poor, who was "in love" with nature and whom John Paul II proclaimed as the patron of stewards of creation?

Francis is the very pontiff who stated, "God entrusted us with the miracle of creation, not to exploit but to love and bring to perfection." He added, "We destroy nature without realizing that we're leaving ourselves with a desert, not a garden."[3]

I remember that in a documentary released at the end of March 2013, an Italian priest was interviewed on the day of Pope Francis's inauguration Mass, and brimming with enthusiasm he said, "*Questo papa non solo cambierá la chiesa cambierá il mondo*" (This pope will change not only the church but also the world).[4] Only six days had passed since the conclave, and Francis had shown just the first few signs of his papal style, but they were enough to spur that priest to proclaim his faith and hope in a better future in the hands of the new pontiff.

I also remember that after his first three months, people began saying that Pope Francis's honeymoon with the people would soon be over. A mistaken prediction: time passed, and the enthusiasm is only increasing. According to a December 2014 survey conducted in Italy for *La Repubblica* newspaper by Demos, the new pontiff had reached an approval rating of 88 percent. While trust in the Church was growing, Italian citizens were losing their trust in political institutions. For example, between 2010 and 2014, the public's faith in the president and in magistrates dropped to 27 percent and 17 percent, respectively.[5]

This rejuvenated Church—one that is inspiring confidence and regaining prominence in the West—is yearning to be heard in the world through a pope who is making a profound impression on Catholics and on all people of goodwill.

3. "Francisco anunció que prepara una encíclica ecológica."
4. *El papa del fin del mundo.*
5. Diamanti, "Partiti, istituzioni, Europa."

Bibliography

Abbott, Walter M., ed. *The Documents of Vatican II: All Sixteen Official Texts Promulgated by the Ecumenical Council 1963-1965*. Translated by Joseph Gallagher et al. New York: America Press, 1966.
Adriance, Madeleine. *Opting for the Poor: Brazilian Catholicism in Transition*. Kansas City: Sheed and Ward, 1986.
Allen, John L., Jr. "CELAM Update: 'Option for the Poor' Alive and Well in Latin America." *National Catholic Reporter*, May 21, 2007. http://ncronline.org/news/celam-update-option-poor-alive-and-well-latin-america.
Alon, Gedaliah. "The Halakah in the Teaching of the Twelve Apostles (*Didache*)." In *The Didache in Modern Research*, edited by Jonathan A. Draper, 165-94. New York: Brill, 1996.
Alva, Reginald. *Mary and the Catholic Charismatic Renewal Movement*. Delhi: Indian Society for Promoting Christian Knowledge, 2012.
Ambrogetti, Francesca. "Pope Leads 'Revolution of Tenderness,' Says Theologian." *Gazzetta del Sud*, March 5, 2014. http://www.gazzettadelsud.it/news/english/82546/Pope-leads—revolution-of-tenderness—says-theologian.html.
Apostoli, Andrew. *Fatima for Today: The Urgent Marian Message of Hope*. San Francisco: Ignatius, 2010.
Aristotle. *Nicomachean Ethics*. Translated by Martin Ostwald. Indianapolis: Bobbs-Merrill, 1962.
Arocho Esteves, Junno. "Neocatechumenal Way Initiators Meet with Pope Francis." *Zenit*, May 20, 2013. http://www.zenit.org/en/articles/neocatechumenal-way-initiators-meet-with-pope-francis.
Baeck, Leo. *The Essence of Judaism*. Translated by Victor Grubwieser and Leonard Pearl. London: Macmillan, 1936.
———. *Judaism and Christianity: Essays*. Translated by Walter Kaufmann. New York: Atheneum, 1970.
Benedict XVI, Pope. "Meeting with the Bishops of Portugal." May 13, 2010. Fátima, Portugal. http://w2.vatican.va/content/benedict-xvi/en/speeches/2010/may/documents/hf_ben-xvi_spe_20100513_vescovi-portogallo.html.
Bennett, Jeffrey S. *When the Sun Danced: Myth, Miracles, and Modernity in Early Twentieth-Century Portugal*. Charlottesville: University of Virginia Press, 2012.

BIBLIOGRAPHY

Benson, Robert Hugh. *Lord of the World*. New York: Dodd, Mead, 1908.

Bergoglio, Jorge Mario. "Evangelizing Implies Apostolic Zeal." Intervention given during 2013 pre-conclave General Congregation meetings of the Cardinals in Rome. http://en.radiovaticana.va/storico/2013/03/27/bergoglios_intervention_a_diagnosis_of_the_problems_in_the_church/en1-677269.

———. "For Man." In *A Generative Thought: An Introduction to the Works of Luigi Giussani*, edited by Elisa Buzzi, 79–83. Montreal: McGill-Queen's University Press, 2003.

———. "The Gratitude of Buenos Aires." *Traces* 4 (April 1999) 14–16. http://english.clonline.org/default.asp?id=440&id_n=20152.

———. "Il messaggio di Aparecida ai presbiteri." *RomaSette*, July 7, 2013. http://www.romasette.it/uploads/57f117ce-8c94-24cb.pdf.

———. "Pobres en este mundo, ricos en la fe: A propósito de la figura y el pensamiento del padre Rafael Tello." *Vida Pastoral* 310 (September 2012). http://www.san-pablo.com.ar/vidapastoral/nota.php?id=664.

———. "Ponencia del Sr. Arzobispo en la V Conferencia del C.E.L.A.M." Aparecida, Brazil, May 13–31, 2007. http://www.arzbaires.org.ar/inicio/homilias/homilias2007.htm#Ponencia_del_Sr._Arzobispo_en_la_V_Conferencia_del_C.E.L.A.M__.

Bergoglio, Jorge Mario, and Abraham Skorka. *On Heaven and Earth: Pope Francis on Faith, Family, and the Church in the Twenty-First Century*. Translated by Alejandro Bermudez and Howard Goodman. New York: Image, 2013.

Bianchi, Enrique Ciro. *Pobres en este mundo, ricos en la fe*. Buenos Aires: Agape, 2012.

Binelli, Mark. "Pope Francis: The Times They Are A-Changin'." *Rolling Stone*, January 28, 2014. http://www.rollingstone.com/culture/news/pope-francis-the-times-they-are-a-changin-20140128.

Block, Peter. *Community: The Structure of Belonging*. San Francisco: Berrett-Koehler, 2008.

Boyarin, Daniel. *Dying for God: Martyrdom in Christianity and Judaism*. Stanford: Stanford University Press, 1999.

Buber, Martin. *Two Types of Faith*. Translated by Norman P. Goldhawk. New York: Macmillan, 1951.

Carrón, Julián. Letter from Milan to the Fraternity of CL. October 16, 2013. http://english.clonline.org/default.asp?id=559&id_n=20337.

CBCP News. "Pope Francis' Papacy 'Biggest Challenge' to PH Church—Villegas." July 6, 2014. http://www.cbcpnews.com/cbcpnews/?p=37918.

Chesnut, R. Andrew. "A Preferential Option for the Spirit: The Catholic Charismatic Renewal in Latin America's New Religious Economy." *Latin American Politics and Society* 45 (2003) 55–85.

Chua-Eoan, Howard, and Elizabeth Dias. "Pope Francis, the People's Pope." *Time*, December 11, 2013. http://poy.time.com/2013/12/11/person-of-the-year-pope-francis-the-peoples-pope/.

Conferencia General del Episcopado Latinoamericano y del Caribe (CELAM). *Concluding Document: Aparecida, 13 a 31 de mayo de 2007*. Bogotá: CELAM, 2008. http://www.aecrc.org/documents/Aparecida-Concluding%20Document.pdf.

Culpepper, R. Alan. "The Johannine *Hypodeigma*: A Reading of John 13." *Semeia* 53 (1991) 133–52.

Diamanti, Ilvo. "Partiti, istituzioni, Europa: La fiducia va a picco, cittadini sempre più soli. Il Papa unica speranza." *La Repubblica*, December 28, 2014. http://www.repubblica.

it/politica/2014/12/28/news/partiti_istituzioni_europa_la_fiducia_va_a_picco_cittadini_sempre_pi_soli_il_papa_unica_speranza-103904923/?ref=search.

Dunn, James D. G. "The Washing of the Disciples' Feet in John 13:1–20." *Zeitschrift für die neutestamentliche Wissenschaft* 61 (1970) 247–52.

El papa del fin del mundo. Documentary. Produced by Anima Films. 2013. Buenos Aires: History Channel Latinoamérica, 2013. Television.

Epstein, Isidore, ed. *The Babylonian Talmud: seder Mo'ed*. London: Soncino, 1938.

Faggioli, Massimo. "Francesco, ritorno al Concilio Vaticano II." *Europa Quotidiano*, March 21, 2013. http://www.europaquotidiano.it/2013/03/21/francesco-ritorno-al-concilio-vaticano-ii.

———. *Pope Francis: Tradition in Transition*. Mahwah, NJ: Paulist, 2015.

———. *Vatican II: The Battle for Meaning*. Mahwah, NJ: Paulist, 2012.

Fagin, Gerald. *Putting on the Heart of Christ*. Chicago: Loyola, 2010.

Fernández, Victor Manuel. "Bergoglio a secas." *Vida Pastoral* 318 (June 2013). http://www.sanpablo.com.ar/vidapastoral/nota.php?id=738.

Fernández, Victor Manuel, and Paolo Rodari. *El programa del Papa Francisco: ¿Adónde nos quiere llevar?* Buenos Aires: Editorial San Pablo, 2014.

Finkelstein, Louis. *Siphre ad Deuteronomium*. New York: Jewish Theological Seminary of America, 1969.

Flannery, Edward H. *The Anguish of the Jews*. New York: Macmillan, 1979.

Flusser, David. *Judaism and the Origins of Christianity*. Jerusalem: Magnes, 1988.

"Focolare President Promises Pope Testimony of Joy: Maria Voce among Leaders Who Greeted Francis." Zenit, May 20, 2013. http://www.zenit.org/en/articles/focolare-president-promises-pope-testimony-of-joy.

Ford, Josephine Massyngbaerde. *Redeemer—Friend and Mother: Salvation in Antiquity and in the Gospel of John*. Minneapolis: Fortress, 1997.

Francis, Pope. "Address on the Vigil of Pentecost with the Ecclesial Movements." May 18, 2013. St. Peter's Square, Rome. http://w2.vatican.va/content/francesco/en/speeches/2013/may/documents/papa-francesco_20130518_veglia-pentecoste.html.

———. "Audience with the College of Cardinals." March 15, 2013, Clementine Hall. https://w2.vatican.va/content/francesco/en/speeches/2013/march/documents/papa-francesco_20130315_cardinali.html.

———. "Homily for the Chrism Mass." March 28, 2013, St. Peter's Basilica, Rome. http://w2.vatican.va/content/francesco/en/homilies/2013/documents/papa-francesco_20130328_messa-crismale.html.

———. *The Joy of the Gospel (Evangelii gaudium): Apostolic Exhortation*. Rome: Libreria Editrice Vaticana, 2013. http://w2.vatican.va/content/francesco/en/apost_exhortations/documents/papa-francesco_esortazione-ap_20131124_evangelii-gaudium.html.

———. "Meeting with the Bishops of Brazil: Address of Pope Francis—Apostolic Journey to Rio de Janeiro on the Occasion of the XXVIII World Youth Day." July 28, 2013, Rio de Janeiro, Brazil. http://w2.vatican.va/content/francesco/en/speeches/2013/july/documents/papa-francesco_20130727_gmg-episcopato-brasile.html.

———. "On the Path of Jesus: The Pope's Mass at Santa Marta." *L'Osservatore Romano*, September 28, 2013. http://www.osservatoreromano.va/en/news/on-the-path-of-jesus.

BIBLIOGRAPHY

———. "Solemnity of Pentecost; Holy Mass with the Ecclesial Movements." Homily given in St. Peter's Square, May 19, 2013. http://w2.vatican.va/content/francesco/en/homilies/2013/documents/papa-francesco_20130519_omelia-pentecoste.html.

"Francisco anunció que prepara una encíclica ecológica." *El País*, July 28, 2014. http://www.elpais.com.uy/mundo/francisco-anuncio-que-prepara-enciclica.html.

"Full Transcript of Pope's In-Flight Press Remarks Released." Catholic News Agency, August 5, 2013. http://www.catholicnewsagency.com/news/full-transcript-of-popes-in-flight-press-remarks-released.

Gagliarducci, Andrea. "Pope's Words in Interview May Not Have Been His Own, Scalfari Says." Catholic News Agency, November 21, 2013. http://www.catholicnewsagency.com/news/popes-words-in-interview-may-not-have-been-his-own-scalfari-says.

Gaillardetz, Richard. "Francis Wishes to Release Vatican II's Bold Vision from Captivity." *National Catholic Reporter*, September 25, 2013. http://ncronline.org/news/vatican/francis-wishes-release-vatican-iis-bold-vision-captivity.

Galli, Carlos María. "Introducción." In Eduardo Pironio, *Signos en la Iglesia latinoamericana: Evangelización y liberación*. Buenos Aires: Editorial Guadalupe, 2012.

———. "Papa Francisco." *Vida Pastoral* 328 (May 2014) 14.

———. "Ternura, alegría, conversion y reforma: la teología pastoral de Francisco en *Evangelii gaudium*." Printed conference notes, Archdiocesan Seminary (De Voto) of Buenos Aires, June 6, 2014.

García, Rocío Lancho. "Pope to Catholic Charismatic Renewal: Tell Them I Love Them Very Much." Zenit, April 30, 2013. http://www.zenit.org/en/articles/pope-to-catholic-charismatic-renewal-tell-them-i-love-them-very-much.

Gibbs, Nancy. "Pope Francis, the Choice." *Time*, December 11, 2013. http://poy.time.com/2013/12/11/pope-francis-the-choice/.

Giussani, Luigi. "Communion and Liberation." In *The Ecclesial Movements in the Pastoral Concern of the Bishops*, 154–58. Vatican City: Pontifical Council for the Laity, 2000.

———. *The Religious Sense*. Translated by John Zucchi. Montreal: McGill-Queen's University Press, 1997.

Glatz, Carol, and Cindy Wooden. "Citing Health Reasons, Pope Benedict Announces He Will Resign." Catholic News Service, February 11, 2013. http://www.catholicnews.com/services/englishnews/2013/citing-health-reasons-pope-benedict-announces-he-will-resign-cns-1300566.cfm.

Ha'Am, Ahad. "Al shtei ha-se'ipim." In vol. 4 of *Al Parshat drakhim*. Berlin: Jüdischer Verlag, 1930.

Hafiz, Yasmine. "Pope Francis Named Man of the Year by *Vanity Fair Italia*." *Huffington Post*, July 10, 2013. http://www.huffingtonpost.com/2013/07/10/pope-francis-man-of-the-year-vanity-fair-italia_n_3572939.html.

HaLevi, Ḥayim David. "Darkei Shalom." *Teḥumin* 9, 5748 (1988).

Hanna, Tony. *New Ecclesial Movements: Communion and Liberation, Neo-Catechumenal Way, Charismatic Renewal*. New York: Alba House, 2006.

Harnack, Adolf von. *What Is Christianity?* Translated by Thomas Bailey Saunders. New York: Harper, 1957.

"Havana Prelate Shares Notes from Cardinal Bergoglio's Pre-conclave Speech: Argentine Archbishop Warned against a 'Worldly Church.'" Zenit, March 26, 2013. http://www.zenit.org/en/articles/havana-prelate-shares-notes-from-cardinal-bergoglio-s-pre-conclave-speech.

Heifetz, Ronald, et al. *The Practice of Adaptive Leadership: Tools and Tactics for Changing Your Organization and the World*. Cambridge: Cambridge Leadership Associates, 2009.

Herzog, HaRav Itzhak Isaac HaLevi. "Zekhuiot HaMiu'tim LeFi HaHalakhah." *Tehumin* 2, 5741 (1981).

Heschel, Abraham Joshua. "No Religion Is an Island." In *Moral Grandeur and Spiritual Audacity*, edited by Susannah Heschel, 235–50. New York: Farrar, Straus and Giroux, 1996.

———. "On Improving Catholic-Jewish Relations." http://www.ajcarchives.org/AJC_DATA/Files/6A4.PDF.

Higger, Michael, ed. *Masekhtot Kalah: ve-hen masekhet Kalah, masekhet Kalah rabati*. New York: Hotsa'at "De-be Rabanan", 1936.

Hultgren, Arland. "The Johannine Footwashing (John 13:1–11) as Symbol of Eschatological Hospitality." *New Testament Studies* 28 (1982) 539–46.

Huppke, Rex. "Lessons in Leadership from Pope Francis." *Chicago Tribune*, November 4, 2013. http://articles.chicagotribune.com/2013-11-04/business/ct-biz-1104-work-advice-huppke-20131104_1_leadership-style-first-jesuit-pope-jorge-mario-bergoglio.

Ignatius of Loyola. *The Spiritual Exercises of Saint Ignatuis of Loyola*. Translated by Elder Mullan. 1914. Reprint, Grand Rapids: Christian Classics Ethereal Library, 1990.

Ignatius of Loyola. *The Autobiography of St. Ignatius*. Edited by J. F. X. O'Connor. New York: Benziger Brothers, 1900.

"Jesus' Cross Invites Us to Be Smitten by His Love, Pope Says." Catholic News Agency, July 26, 2013. http://www.catholicnewsagency.com/news/jesus-cross-invites-us-to-be-smitten-by-his-love-pope-says/.

John Paul II, Pope. "Homily at the Mass for Participants at the Congress of 'Movements in the Church.'" *Insegnamenti* 4/II (1981) 305–6.

———. *Christifideles laici: Post-Synodal Apostolic Exhortation*. Rome: Libreria Editrice Vaticana, 1998. http://w2.vatican.va/content/john-paul-ii/en/apost_exhortations/documents/hf_jp-ii_exh_30121988_christifideles-laici.html.

———. "Message for the World Congress of Ecclesial Movements and New Communities." May 27, 1998. https://w2.vatican.va/content/john-paul-ii/en/speeches/1998/may/documents/hf_jp-ii_spe_19980527_movimenti.html.

———. "Speech of the Holy Father Pope John Paul II: Meeting with Ecclesial Movements and New Communities." May 30, 1998. http://w2.vatican.va/content/john-paul-ii/en/speeches/1998/may/documents/hf_jp-ii_spe_19980530_riflessioni.html.

John XXIII, Pope. "Pope John's Opening Speech to the Council." October 11, 1962. http://www.christusrex.org/www1/CDHN/v2.html.

Kasper, Walter Cardinal. "Foreword." In *Christ Jesus and the Jewish People Today: New Explorations of Theological Interrelationships*, edited by Philip A. Cunningham et al., x–xviii. Grand Rapids: Eerdmans, 2011.

Kentenich, Joseph. *Forming the New Person: Pedagogical Conferences 1951*. Waukesha, WI: Schoenstatt Fathers, 2004.

Klausner, Joseph. *MiYeshu 'ad Paulus*. Tel Aviv: Mada, 1939–40.

Larraquy, Marcelo. *Recen por él: La historia jamás contada del hombre que desafía los secretos del Vaticano*. Buenos Aires: Sudamericana, 2013.

Leahy, Brendan. *Ecclesial Movements and Communities: Origins, Significance, and Issues*. Hyde Park, NY: New City, 2011.

BIBLIOGRAPHY

Lowney, Chris. *Pope Francis: Why He Leads the Way He Leads; Lessons from the First Jesuit Pope*. Chicago: Loyola, 2013.

Lubac, Henri de. *The Splendour of the Church*. Translated by Michael Mason. New York: Sheed and Ward, 1956.

Malbim, Me'ir Leyb ben Yeḥi'el Mikha'el. *Sifra de-ve Rav: hu sefer Torat kohanim 'im perush ha-Torah 'eha-mits'ah*. Bucharest: Zornal Natsional, 1860.

Manson, Jamie. "One of Pope Francis' Allegiances Might Tell Us Something about the Church's Future." *National Catholic Reporter*, March 15, 2013. https://www.ncronline.org/blogs/grace-margins/one-pope-francis-allegiances-might-tell-us-something-about-churchs-future.

Markham, Donna J. *Spiritlinking Leadership: Working through Resistance to Organizational Change*. New York: Paulist, 1999.

Martin, James. "His Way of Proceeding: How Might Jesuit Spirituality Influence Pope Francis' Papacy?" *America*, April 29, 2013, 16–18.

Maurer, Susan A. *The Spirit of Enthusiasm: A History of the Catholic Charismatic Movement, 1967–2000*. Lanham, MD: University Press of America, 2010.

McFague, Sallie. *Models of God: Theology for an Ecological, Nuclear Age*. Philadelphia: Fortress, 1987.

Mejía, Jorge Cardenal. *Una presencia en el Concilio: Crónicas y apuntes del Concilio Vaticano II*. Buenos Aires: Agape, 2009.

Midrash Rabah. Vilna: Romm, 1878.

Niehaus, Jonathan. *New Vision and Life: The Founding of Schoenstatt (1912–1919)*. 2nd ed. Waukesha, WI: Schoenstatt Fathers, 2004.

Orthodox Union Institute for Public Affairs. "Statement by Dr. David Berger regarding the *New York Times* ad by Dabru Emet." September 14, 2000. http://advocacy.ou.org/2000/statement_by_dr_david_berger_regarding_the_new_york_times_ad_by_dabru_emet.

Paul VI, Pope. *Nostra Aetate: Declaration on the Relation of the Church to Non-Christian Religions*. October 28, 1965. http://www.vatican.va/archive/hist_councils/ii_vatican_council/documents/vat-ii_decl_19651028_nostra-aetate_en.html.

Pawlikoski, John T. "Historical Memory and Christian-Jewish Relations." In *Christ Jesus and the Jewish People Today: New Explorations of Theological Interrelationships*, edited by Philip A. Cunningham et al., 14–30. Grand Rapids: Eerdmans, 2011.

Piqué, Elisabetta. *Francisco: Vida y Revolución*. Buenos Aires: Editorial El Ateneo, 2013.

Pironio, Eduardo. *La iglesia en América Latina*. Buenos Aires: Editora Patria Grande, 1972.

"Pope Francis' Address to the Participants [of the] International Meeting for Peace [Organized] by the Sant'Egidio Community." Zenit, September 30, 2013. http://www.zenit.org/en/articles/pope-francis-address-to-the-participants-international-meeting-for-peace-by-the-sant-egidio.

"Pope Francis Declares Sainthood of Early Jesuit, Peter Faber." CNA/EWTN News, December 17, 2013. http://www.catholicnewsagency.com/news/pope-francis-declares-sainthood-of-early-jesuit-peter-faber/.

"Pope Francis' Homily at Mass in the Church of the Gesu." Zenit, January 3, 2014. http://www.zenit.org/en/articles/pope-francis-homily-at-mass-in-the-church-of-the-gesu.

"Pope Francis Receives Neocatechumenal Way Initiators." Zenit, September 5, 2013. http://www.zenit.org/en/articles/pope-francis-receives-neocatechumenal-way-initiators.

"Pope Francis to the Youth and to the Aged: Do Not Allow Yourselves to Be Marginalized." Vatican Radio, July 25, 2013. http://www.news.va/en/news/pope-francis-to-the-youth-and-to-the-aged-do-not-a.

Prades López, Javier. "The Life of the Church: The Sacramental Method of Evangelization." In *New Religious Movements in the Catholic Church*, edited by Michael A. Hayes, 61–102. London: Burns & Oates, 2005.

Premat, Silvina. "The Attraction of the Cardinal." *Traces* (June 2001). http://english.clonline.org/default.asp?id=440&id_n=20151.

Ratzinger, Joseph. "Ecclesial Movements and Their Place in Theology." In *New Outpourings of the Spirit: Movements in the Church*, translated by Michael J. Miller and Henry Taylor, 17–62. San Francisco: Ignatius, 2007.

———. "The Movements, the Church, the World: Dialogue with Joseph Cardinal Ratzinger." In *New Outpourings of the Spirit: Movements in the Church*, translated by Michael J. Miller and Henry Taylor, 65–117. San Francisco: Ignatius, 2007.

Riccardi, Andrea. "St. Egidio Community." In *The Ecclesial Movements in the Pastoral Concern of the Bishops*, 169. Vatican City: Pontifical Council for the Laity, 2000.

Ringe, Sharon H. *Wisdom's Friends: Community and Christology in the Fourth Gospel*. Louisville: Westminster John Knox, 1999.

Rocca, Francis X. "Pope Francis Discovers Charismatic Movement a Gift to the Whole Church." Catholic News Service, August 9, 2013. http://www.catholicnews.com/services/englishnews/2013/pope-francis-discovers-charismatic-movement-a-gift-to-the-whole-church.cfm.

Rodari, Paolo, and Andrea Tornielli. *Attacco a Ratzinger*. Milan: Piemme, 2010.

Rodríguez Maradiaga, Oscar Andrés. "The Importance of the New Evangelization." Keynote speech at the Synod Closing Assembly, Miami, Florida, October 28, 2013. http://www.miamiarch.org/CatholicDiocese.php?op=Article_13102810144642.

Rubin, Sergio, and Francesca Ambrogetti. *El jesuita: Conversaciones con el Cardenal Jorge Mario Bergolio, S.J.* Buenos Aires: Vergara, 2010.

———. *Pope Francis: Conversations with Jorge Bergoglio*. New York: Putnam, 2013.

Scalfari, Eugenio. "The Pope: How the Church Will Change." *La Repubblica*, October 1, 2013. http://www.repubblica.it/cultura/2013/10/01/news/pope_s_conversation_with_scalfari_english-67643118/.

Scannone, Juan Carlos. "Perspectivas eclesiológicas de la Teología del Pueblo en la Argentina." http://geocities.com/teologialatina/.

Schneiders, Sandra. "A Community of Friends (John 13:1–20)." In *Written That You May Believe: Encountering Jesus in the Fourth Gospel*, 184–201. Rev. ed. New York: Crossroad, 2003.

Schüssler Fiorenza, Elisabeth. "'Waiting at Table': A Critical Feminist Theological Reflection on Diakonia." In *Concilium 198: Diakonia; Church for the Others*, edited by Norbert Greinacher and Norbert Mette, 84–94. Edinburgh: T. & T. Clark, 1988.

Senge, Peter, et al. *Presence: Human Purpose and the Field of the Future*. New York: Doubleday, 2004.

Soloveichik, Meir. "How Soloveitchik Saw Interreligious Dialogue." *Forward*, April 25, 2003. http://forward.com/opinion/8692/how-soloveitchik-saw-interreligious-dialogue/.

Spadaro, Antonio. "A Big Heart Open to God: The Exclusive Interview with Pope Francis." *America*, September 30, 2013. http://americamagazine.org/pope-interview.

———. "Wake Up the World: Conversation with Pope Francis about the Religious Life." Translated by Donald Maldari. *La Civiltà Cattolica*, January 3, 2014. http://

onlineministries.creighton.edu/CollaborativeMinistry/PopeFrancis/Wake_up_the_world-2.pdf.

Spink, Kathryn. *The Miracle, the Message, the Story: Jean Vanier and L'Arche*. Mahwah, NJ: Hiddenspring, 2006.

Tello, Rafael. *Pueblo y cultura popular*. Buenos Aires: Fundación Saracho, 2014.

Theodor, Julius, and Chanoch Albeck. *Midrash Bereshit rabah: al pi ketav-yad ba-British Muzeʼon im shinui noshaʼot mi-shemoneh kitve yad aḥerim u-madpusim rishonim u-ferush Minḥat Yehudah*. Jerusalem: Sifre Vahrman, 1965.

Tornielli, Andrea. "Never Be Afraid of Tenderness." *La Stampa/Vatican Insider*, December 16, 2013. http://vaticaninsider.lastampa.it/en/the-vatican/detail/articolo/30620/.

Vallely, Paul. *Pope Francis: Untying the Knots*. London: Bloomsbury, 2013.

Vanier, Jean. "Seek Out the Weak and the Excluded." *U.S. Catholic* 78.5 (2013) 18–19.

Vatican Council II. *Decree Ad Gentes on the Mission Activity of the Church*. Homebush, NSW: Society of St. Paul, 1965. http://www.vatican.va/archive/hist_councils/ii_vatican_council/documents/vat-ii_decree_19651207_ad-gentes_en.html.

———. *Documentos del Vaticano II*. Madrid: Biblioteca de Autores Cristianos, 1972.

Wheatley, Margaret J. *Leadership and the New Science: Discovering Order in a Chaotic World*. 3rd ed. San Francisco: Berrett-Koehler, 2006.

Whitehead, Charles. *What Is the Nature of the Catholic Charismatic Renewal?* Locust Grove, VA: Chariscenter, 2003.

Winfield, Nicole. "Pope Francis Washes Feet of Young Detainees in Ritual." *Huffington Post*, March 28, 2013. http://www.usatoday.com/story/news/world/2013/03/28/pope-frances-washes-feet/2028595/.

Yuval, Israel Jacob. *Two Nations in Your Womb*. 3rd ed. Tel Aviv: Am Oved, 2000.

Subject Index

anti-Judaism, xiii, 27–28, 31
anti-Semitism, xiii, 24–28
Aparecida Conference, xiv, 36, 44, 47–50, 56, 61, 63, 65, 66
Aparecida document, 7, 44, 94
apostles, 12, 15, 20, 21
    lack of hierarchy among, 16
Argentina, x, xiv, 35–38, 41–44, 46, 55, 56, 92, 94–95, 102, 113
Argentine liberation theology, 43–44
atheism, 19, 23, 64

Benedict XVI, Pope, xi, xv, 1–3, 48, 56, 70, 72, 92, 101, 105, 109
    resignation of, 1, 40, 53, 86, 98

Caritas in veritate, 77
cardinals, xi, 2–5, 40, 66, 87, 108, 112
Catholic Action, 42
Catholic charismatics, 47, 75
Catholic Charismatic Movement in Latin America, 75
Catholic Charismatic Renewal (CCR), 72, 73, 74–76
Catholic Social Doctrine, 36, 41, 42
Catholic University of Argentina, 44
Catholicism
    in Latin America, 40–42
    and other religions, 91
    and Second Vatican Council, x, 41, 43, 52, 72, 96
    teachings of, 41
CELAM, 42, 44, 48, 56, 94n6
charism, 74–76, 77, 79, 82, 85, 91
Christianity
    and joy, 77
    and Judaism, 24–34, 90
    and anti-Semitism, 24, 27–28
    and Nazism, xiii, 25, 27, 34
    relationships in, xii
    and tradition, 104
clericalism, xv, 38, 46, 49, 50
Church, the
    centralization, 21
    cultural revolution in, xvii, 109
    decentralization, 20
    future of, 86–97
    hierarchy, lack of, 20
    in Latin America, 36, 40–42, 48, 75–76 (*see also* Latin American Church)
    missionary, 46, 47, 49, 50–51, 66, 72, 81–82, 83, 85
    missionary identity, 41, 48, 49, 51
    reform in, x, xv, xvii, 35–52, 58, 61, 90, 92–93, 101, 111
    women in the, 21, 49, 61, 79n, 96, 109
Cold War, 38, 43
Communion and Liberation (CL) Movement, 70, 72, 73, 79, 81, 84
    See also Giussani, Luigi
communism, 43, 44

SUBJECT INDEX

community
 and disciples, 16, 17
 and Jesus, 18, 20
 Johannine, 16
Conference of Latin American Bishops.
 See CELAM
Curia
 reform of, xi, 2, 109

Dabru Emet, 26–29
discernment, xi, 4, 5, 39, 40
 five criteria for, 71
 Ignatian, 39, 53–69
disciples
 as apostles, 20
 community of, 16, 17
 equal status of, 16
 and foot washing, 11, 12
 hierarchy, lack of, 16, 20
 and Jesus, 12, 14–17
 and Mary, 82
 missionary, 7, 49, 64
 women as, 21
diversity, 10, 85
Dives in misericordia, 6
divine name, 18
Don Bosco, 36

Ecumenism, xv, 47, 83, 90, 113
Evangelii gaudium, 19, 20, 21, 22, 23, 45,
 48, 60, 61, 62n, 63, 64n, 68n, 70,
 74, 78, 79, 82, 85n, 103
Evangelii nuntiandi, 41, 48, 50
evangelization, 20, 45, 78, 103
 in Argentina, 95
 "Marian style," 82, 83, 85
 New Evangelization, 8, 45, 70, 72, 75,
  76, 78, 81, 82, 85
Extraordinary Synod of Bishops, 76

Fatima, 84
 Our Lady of, 73, 85
 movement, 84
 World Apostolate of Fatima, 73, 84
Favre, Peter, 68–69
Francis, Pope

as Archbishop of Buenos Aires, xiv,
 22, 35, 38, 44, 46–47, 55, 61, 108
and Argentine liberation theology,
 35, 43–45
and Aparecida, xiv, 7, 44, 47–50, 56,
 61, 63, 65, 66, 94
and atheism, 19, 23, 64
choice of name, xi, 5, 53, 88–90, 93,
 110, 114
and charity, xvi, 39, 87
and divine mercy, 6–7, 22, 23, 61, 62,
 80, 100, 104
and doubt, xv, 59
and ecclesial movements, xv, 70–85
and *Evangelii gaudium*, 19, 20, 21, 22,
 23, 45, 48, 60, 61, 62n, 63, 64n,
 68n, 70, 74, 78, 79, 82, 85n, 103
"first global pope," 112
and foot washing, xii, 9, 18–20
and the Gospel of John, xii, 10, 11–
 19, 22
and humility, xiv, 19, 101
as immigrant, x, xiii–xiv, 36–37, 54
and Ignatian spirituality, x–xii, xiii, 6,
 7, 38, 39, 53–69
and interfaith dialogue, xii
and interreligious dialogue, xiii, xiv,
 xv, 37, 47, 77, 90–91, 93, 113
as a Jesuit, x, xiv, xv, 35, 37–40, 43, 46,
 52, 54–56, 67, 68, 79, 89, 108
and joy, x, xv, 22, 67, 77
leadership style, xii, xvi, 9–10, 18–19,
 21–23, 40
and love, xii, xiii, xvii, 39, 58, 109–
 110
and Mary, xv, 73, 76, 82–85
as missionary pope, 7, 20, 47, 48,
 49, 50–51, 64, 66, 71, 76, 82, 83,
 104–5
and pastoral ministry, 37, 47, 64, 104
and the poor, xvi, 3, 5, 6, 36–37, 38,
 44, 46, 50, 51, 58, 64, 65, 71,
 72–73, 78, 79, 87, 89, 93–94, 96,
 102, 108, 110
populist approach, xi, 5, 6
and predecessors, xv, 8, 70–72, 79, 92,
 105, 109, 112

SUBJECT INDEX

and reform, xvii, 35–36, 40, 48–52, 58, 61, 90, 92–93, 101, 103, 107–14
and traditionalist movements, 41, 47
urban experience, xiv, 37, 112
and women in the Church, 21, 49, 96, 109
Francis of Assisi, Saint, xi, 79, 85, 88, 90, 110, 114
freedom, 4, 5, 22, 39, 40, 53, 56, 57, 105, 110
friendship, xii, xiii, 16, 20
   freely chosen, 17
   and Pope Francis, 37
   and service, 15
Focolare Movement, 72, 73, 77, 84
foot washing, xii, 9–23

Gaudium et spes, 40
Gaudium magnum, 87
gender, 18, 50, 96
Gentile Christians, 30, 31, 32, 90n
Gera, Lucio, 43–44
Giussani, Luigi, 70, 73, 78, 79–82
   See also Communion and Liberation (CL)
Gospel of John, xii, 10, 22, 28, 77, 81, 83, 85
   and foot washing, 11–18, 19
governance
   ecclesiastical, xi, 2
   sharing, 20

homosexuality, 60, 96, 109

Ignatius of Loyola, Saint, x, 39, 89
   Spiritual Exercises of, xiv, 7, 39, 54, 56, 57–68, 89
Ignatian spirituality, x, xiii, 6, 38, 39, 40, 54, 56, 57–68
   See also discernment
interfaith dialogue, xii, 29
International Meeting for Peace, 77, 78n31
interreligious dialogue, xv, 29, 47, 77, 90–91, 93, 113

Jesuit Order, x, xiii, xv, 54, 67
   and Pope Francis, xiv, 35, 37–40, 43, 46, 54–56, 68, 89
   See also Inatian spirituality; Ignatius of Loyola
Jesus, 20–23, 34, 51, 62, 79, 81, 83, 104
   and baptizing ministry, 13
   and death, xii, 11–14, 17, 25, 82
   and foot washing, 10–11, 12, 15–17, 19
   and the Gospel of John, 10, 18
   love for all, 11, 12, 63
   teachings, 9, 14, 17, 30, 32, 60
Jewish-Christian relationships, xii, 24–34
   and anti-Semitism, 24–28
   and Dabru Emet, 26–29
   and dialogue, xiii, 13, 24–34, 77, 91
   and Nazism, xiii, 25, 27, 34
   and *Nostra aetete*, 24n, 25–26, 28, 34, 90
   and Pope Francis, xii, 37, 47, 90–91
Johannine
   chronology, 14
   community, 16
   foot washing, 11n10
   Jesus, 16, 20, 22
John the Baptist, 13, 14
John Paul I, Pope 100
John Paul II, Pope, 1, 2, 6, 8, 26, 42, 48, 56, 70–72, 77, 79, 112, 114
John XXIII, Pope, xv, 25, 26, 41, 90, 93, 108
joy, x, 22–23, 57, 67, 77, 82, 87
Judaism, 26, 29, 113
   and roots of Christianity, 30–32, 90

Kentenich, Fr. Joseph, 76

Latin America, x, xiv, 37, 41, 47, 75, 113
Latin American Catholicism, 40, 41, 42, 76
Latin American Church, 42, 48
   and Cardijn, Cardinal Joseph, 42
   and the Second Vatican Council, 40
   and traditionalist movement, 41
   and Young Christian Workers, 42

SUBJECT INDEX

leadership, xi–xii, xv, 49–50, 59
   and diversity, 10
   and foot washing, xii
   of Jesus, 14–15, 18–19
   new models of, 10
   of Pope Francis, xiv, xvi, 9–10, 21–23, 40
   as service, 15
   and timing, 13
love, 6, 49, 50, 80, 82, 104, 114
   divine, xii, 11–20, 22–23, 63, 67, 97
Lumen gentium, 40, 49, 79n37

Mary
   and evangelization, 73, 82–85
   as the "great missionary", xv, 73, 84
Maimonides, 34
mercy, 6, 14, 50, 61, 63, 67, 80, 97, 100, 104
   God's, xii, xiv, 6–7, 19, 22–23, 49, 57, 62
Middle East, 113
movements, 42, 75, 92
   Ecclesial, xv, 70–74, 78–79, 84–85
   Focolare, 73, 77, 84
   L'Arche, 78, 83
   lay, 71, 73
   Marian, 76, 84
   modern, 71, 76, 77, 79, 83–84
   Neocatechumenal Way, 73, 76–77
   Sant'Egidio, 73, 77–78
   Schoenstatt, 73, 76, 84
   traditionalist, 41
   See also Catholic Charismatic Renewal (CCR); Communion and Liberation (CL) Movement

New Testament, 28, 29, 49
Nostra aetate, 25, 26, 28, 34, 90
   approval of, 25
   and Islam, 26
   and John XXIII, 90
   and Rabbi Heschel, 26

pastoral conversion, xvi, 48–50, 61, 100, 102, 104–5

Pauline Christianity, 30
Paul VI, Pope, 25, 42, 112
   Evangelii nuntiandi, 41, 48, 50
   Populorum progressio, 41
peace, 27, 58, 67, 77, 78, 83, 84–85, 88, 110, 113
Peronism, xiv, 36, 38
Pironio, Cardinal Eduardo, 42, 44
Pius XII, Pope, 38, 108
   and the Shoah, 25
Pontifical Council for the Laity, 71, 75, 84
Pontifical Council for Promoting the New Evangelization, 75, 78
populism, 37
poverty, x, xvi, 41, 65, 67, 77, 80, 83, 87, 88, 93–94, 102, 103, 112–13
   and wealth, 112

reform, x, xi, xvii, 2, 35–36, 40, 48, 50, 51, 58, 61, 90, 101, 109, 111
   liturgical, xv, 92–93
   See also Second Vatican Council
renewal, xiii, xvii, 23, 30–31, 33, 51–52, 79, 92, 96, 103, 108, 111
revolution, x, xvii, 40, 43, 94, 109–12

Salesians, 36
Second Vatican Council, x, 25, 38, 41, 42, 43, 52, 71–72, 77, 96
   and charism, 74
   and *Gaudium et spes*, 40
   and Latin American bishops, 36, 40
   and Second General Conference, 40
service, 7, 15, 36, 51, 73, 83, 92
   Pope Francis and, 23, 44, 46
   and friendship, 15–17
   models of, 11, 15–16
   to the Church, 74, 75
sex
   celibacy, 51
   homosexuality, 60, 96, 109
   issues regarding, 110
   and morality, 49
   and orientation, 51
social justice, 37, 110
Synod of Bishops, 56, 76

Synod of Bishops on the Laity, 71
Synod on the Family
   2014, 51
   2015, 8, 20, 109
Synod on Justice, 41
Synoptic Gospels, 12, 14, 16, 30

Talmud, 31–32
Tello, Rafael, 43–45, 95

Torah, 27, 34
   Law of the, 32

women
   and the Church, 21, 49, 96, 109
   and foot-washing, xii, 9
World Youth Day, xii, 22, 54, 62, 75, 96

Young Catholic Workers, 42

Scripture Index

Exod
3:14	18
12:46	14

Lev
25:36	33n27

Job
28	18

Prov
1–9	18
3:17	18n24
3:18	18n24
8.7	18n24
8:32	18n24
8:34	18n24
8:35	18n24
8:38	18n24

Zeph
3:9	34

Wis
6–10	18
6:22	18n24
7:26	18n24
18:34	18n24

Sir
1	18
4:11–19	18
6:18–31	18
6:26	18n24
14:20–15	18
24:17	18n24
24:19	18n24
24:21	18n24
44:16	14

Bar
3:9–4:4	18

2 Macc
6:18–31	14
6:19	14
6:27–28	14

4 Macc

17:22–23	14

Matt

5:14	72
5:17ff	32
16:19	16

Mark

1:19	16n19
1:29	16n19
5:37	16n19
6:37	62
8:32–33	17
9:2	16n19
13:3	16n19
14:33	16n19

Luke

1:39	83
4:18	79
8:3	21

John

1:11	12
1:14	16
1:18	13, 13n13
1:29	14
1:36	14
2:1–11	83
2:4	13n14
3:14–16	11
3:26	13
4	15
4:21	13n14
4:23	13n14
4:42	15
5:25	13n14
5:28–29	13n14
6:35	18
6:48	18
6:51	11
6:67	12, 16n18
6:70	12, 16n18
6:71	16n18
7:30	13n14
7:37–39	11
8:12	18
8:20	13n14
8:43–47	28
8:59	13
9:5	18
10:3–4	12
10:7	18
10:9	18
10:10	22
10:11	11, 18
10:17–18	14
10:31	13
10:39	13
10:40	13
11	13
11:8	13
11:16	13
11:53	13
12:24	11
13:1–20	11
13:1	11,12,13,14
13:8	17
13:12–20	14
13:15	14
13:16	12,15, 17
13:19	17–18
13:23	12, 16
13:34	15
14:6	18
14:27	85
15	15
15:1	18
15:13	15
15:14	15
15:15	xii, 17
16:2	13n14
16:20	22
16:25	13n14
16:32	13n14
17:21	77

19:26	16, 82–83
19:30	12
19:33	14
20:8	16
20:21	15
20:24	12, 16n18
21:5	xii

Acts

1:14	82
18:1–4	21

Rom

7:1	31
8:28	85
16:1–2	21
16:3–5	21
16:7	21

1 Cor

12	74n20
13	74n20

Gal

3:28	16

Phil

4:7	85

Rev

2:29	61
12	85
22:17	75

www.ingramcontent.com/pod-product-compliance
Lightning Source LLC
Chambersburg PA
CBHW031502160426
43195CB00010BB/1069